WILL
YOU?
I
DO!

Instant
Weddings

Instant Weddings

From "Will You?" to "I Do!"
in Four Months or Less

By Jennifer L. Shawne
Illustrations by Mary Lynn Blasutta

CHRONICLE BOOKS
SAN FRANCISCO

Text copyright © 2004 by Jennifer L. Shawne. Illustrations copyright © 2004 by
Mary Lynn Blasutta. All rights reserved. No part of this book may be reproduced
in any form without written permission from the publisher.

Library of Congress Cataloging-in-Publication Data available.

ISBN: 0-8118-3687-8

Manufactured in China.

Design by
Amy Quinlivan Design Inc.

Typeset by Smart Set, Incorporated

Distributed in Canada by Raincoast Books
9050 Shaughnessy Street
Vancouver, British Columbia V6P 6E5

10 9 8 7 6 5 4 3 2

Chronicle Books LLC
85 Second Street
San Francisco, California 94105

www.chroniclebooks.com

ACKNOWLEDGMENTS

Writing this book would not have been possible if the following people had not generously shared their time and ideas: Kim Stevens of Living Room Events, Ken Swyt of Ken Swyt Design, photographers Michael Rauner and Daniel Gohstand, and Jen DePatta of Sparkle Events — all in the San Francisco Bay Area; Glenna Tooman of Memory Makers Event Planning in Boise, Idaho; Jerry Monaghan, president of the Association of Bridal Consultants; Laura Holycross of Event Design Studio in Los Angeles; Lanitra Johnson of Johnson Events Group in New Orleans; and Vikki Marinich of Las Vegas Weddings by Vikki, who went the extra mile by sharing her own fantastic "Instant Wedding" story for this book.

Many thanks to the couples whose wedding stories are told in this book for allowing me to share their tales with the world, and to the numerous friends and colleagues who offered snippets of advice and support throughout the writing of this book.

Much appreciation to my editor, Mikyla Bruder, and to Leslie Davisson at Chronicle Books, whose professionalism and warm personalities have made working on this project a real pleasure and delight.

Most of all, thanks to my husband, Alan, who encouraged me to write this book, cheering me on until the end, and whom I'd marry three hundred more times if I could.

Table of Contents

Introduction

The authors of today's bridal guides make
many assumptions. They assume you want a gigantic,
froufrou white gown and a wedding day that veers from
tradition in only the subtlest of ways. They assume you'll
be spending a small fortune for your "perfect day," with
only an occasional nod to the budget-challenged bride,
such as "Ask a friend to do it."

It is totally taken for granted that you will care very
much about doing things the "right" and "proper" way, lest
you come off as some cheap, impolite floozy. Most notably,
these publications dole out reams of advice and pointers
based on the assumption that you have a luxurious twelve
months (or more!) to get all your plans in order before
strutting down the aisle.

Every wedding is unique, as are the circumstances
that give rise to it. And while a whole year is certainly nice
for putting together a celebration of this scale, it's hardly
necessary. Indeed, the "instant wedding" has its own rich
and storied history. Wars from the Christian Crusades to
World War II, and even recent conflicts, have always
produced a batch of fearless "war brides," who marry after
a soldier's summons is issued but before the poor fellow
gets shipped off to the battlefield. Accidents will happen,
and so we have the tradition of the "shotgun wedding,"
where the groom was given the choice of marrying his
pregnant gal or meeting his maker at the hands of the

gal's father. Las Vegas, where no fewer than nine thousand weddings are performed each month, is a tribute to the undying appeal of acting on one's whims and saying "I do" weeks, days, even hours after he or she asks, "Will you?" Happily, the world is a much nicer place for quickly-weds than it has been in years past. Today, countless brides find themselves getting hitched in a hurry—be they unexpectedly expecting, madly in love with a recently deported Italian doctor, taking a toned-down approach to a second wedding, heeding their accountant's or attorney's advice, or simply not about to spend a full year doting over hideous wedding trinkets while screening calls from eager-to-help relatives. While weddings of this kind may certainly come as a surprise to friends and relatives, they no longer come with the negative connotations of coercion and world conflicts they once did. And just because a bride is short on time, this doesn't mean she's also short on imagination, style, dreams, and emotion—nor should her wedding be. Instant weddings are just as romantic, exciting, and crazed down to the last second as weddings that are planned years in advance. Seriously.

This book will provide you with all the standard fare you'd expect from any self-respecting wedding-planning guide—location, dress, flowers, music, shoes, budget, wedding planners, etiquette, lingerie, bridesmaids, strippers, nasty relatives, honeymoon, champagne, trinkets, photography, Web sites, invitations, cakes, pedicures, priests, therapy, birdseed, and let us not forget bubble baths (phew)—but all the advice is tailored to serve the needs of the fast-track couple.

That's important because a wedding planned in four short months will require a different approach than one that's planned over the course of a long year. It's not enough to simply condense the standard twelve-month calendar into a few harried weekends. When time is of the essence, priorities change, as does your schedule. Because popular wedding locations are booked far in advance, it'll require some ingenuity and flexibility on your part to find a great locale. You may have to throw your reception on a Friday instead of a Saturday, or exchange vows at a public park instead of a private chapel. Rather than ordering the perfect dress and waiting months for it to arrive, you'll need to search for off-the-rack or vintage fashions or hit up your mom for her gorgeous gown. Invitations become a top priority so you can give out-of-town guests sufficient time to make their plans. Hoping for a foreign honeymoon? Make sure your passport is up-to-date immediately!

This book will also offer help for situations that don't exactly classify as fairy-tale material but are realities you may have to deal with nonetheless: wedding-day morning sickness, INS hassles, prenuptial PMS, busybody relatives, elopement, and the hidden riches of costume-rental shops. You'll learn about how the wedding industry works and how to make the system work for you. Each chapter will include tips customized to fit small and large budgets, ideas to get your creative juices flowing, and pointers on using the Internet to facilitate planning and communication.

Resources are listed by catagory at the end of the book, giving you immediate access to the information you need. The eight profiles of "instant couples" will give you a sense of how others have approached planning their instant weddings.

If you're reading this book, then presumably you're hoping to take that monumental stroll down the aisle sooner rather than later. A surprise pregnancy or immigration concerns may be dictating your sooner-than-expected wedding date. Perhaps you or someone very close to you is due to move away and you want to have the wedding before he or she leaves. You may have been engaged for months and months and are only now getting around to putting the ceremony and reception together. (Don't feel bad; most couples will tell you that they waited until the last few months to make the bulk of their wedding arrangements.) Or maybe you see no need for an extended engagement period; you know you want to wed, so why not wed now?

In our society, faster is often equated with cheaper and less satisfying. A microwaved dinner is usually inferior to one made from scratch. Service at a quickie oil-change chain is less friendly and personal than what you might expect from your neighborhood mechanic. In other situations, speed is appreciated and comes at a premium— faster Web connections, overnight shipment, and drive-through pharmacies are good examples. With weddings, thank goodness, none of the usual rules apply.

A wedding in the works for a year can be as vulgar and shoddy as a faux designer bag, while one thrown together in a month can be incredibly beautiful and authentic—and vice-versa. Money may be able to buy you the finest linen, the most elaborate hand-written invitations, and a dress that any self-respecting diva would die for, but it can't buy you creativity, supportive family and friends, or, in the Beatles' famous words, love. A wedding that's been organized down to the last detail will be as emotionally powerful for its participants as a quick jog to the courthouse. In fact, a Las Vegas wedding planner I spoke with says her couples are often surprised by the intense feelings they experience during the ceremony, even if it lasts only five minutes and is officiated by a complete stranger.

So, please, set aside any fears you have that your day will be somehow less satisfying because you are short on time. With hard work and imagination, your wedding day will be whatever you want it to be. Ready to get started? Turn the page.

Note: While this book uses the words bride *and* groom *for convenience's sake, it is in no way meant to imply that she's a she and he's a he. The advice herein will be good for all couples looking to make a long-lasting commitment—young or old, gay or straight, single or divorced, richer or poorer—whether their union is recognized by the law or not.*

Countdown Checklist

Let the countdown begin! The following is a checklist of things you'll need to at least consider when planning your wedding. Relevant items from this section will appear at the beginning of each chapter. Although this list begins four months before the big day, feel free to adjust it to match your own schedule and priorities! So if you have just four weeks, you should tackle the things you would four months out one month before the event.

Four months to go . . .

Inform immediate family and close friends of your plans.

Set priorities with groom.

Contact accountants and lawyers, if necessary.

Bookmark relevant Web sites and magazine articles.

Evaluate your finances.

Set a realistic budget.

Ask for money, if needed.

Create a style for the reception.

Hire a wedding coordinator.

Finalize the guest list; check spelling and addresses.

Visit and book reception and ceremony locations.

Pick a venue, if different from reception.

Shop for and buy or order wedding dress.

Choose and buy or order wedding rings.

Three months to go . . .

Communicate key details to family, wedding party, and far-flung guests.

Delegate key tasks to family and wedding party.

Choose an officiant and witness.

Hire the caterer.

Select bridesmaids' dresses.

Order invitations and personalized items.

Book a photographer.

Two months to go . . .

Pick out and order flowers and decorations.

Choose a menu.

Reserve rentals and/or find alternatives.

Pick, buy, or rent groom's and groomsmen's outfits.

Order and send "save the date" cards.

Order thank-you notes.

Register for gifts.

Build a wedding Web site.

Book musicians and other entertainment.

Hire florist and plan flowers.

One month to go . . .

Get marriage license and blood tests (if required).

Choose or write a ceremony script.

Order dessert.

Buy the booze.

Schedule appointments for hair, makeup, nails, and other pampering.

Address and mail invitations.

Arrange to take time off work.

Update passport/visa, if necessary.

Book wedding-day and honeymoon transportation and lodging.

One week to go . . .

Review final ceremony script and details with officiant.

Confirm plans with venues, caterer, rental company, florist, entertainers, bakery.

Get rings sized, if necessary.

Have final dress fitting.

Do practice runs for hair and makeup.

Visit site with photographer and discuss picture list.

Confirm travel plans.

Wrap things up at work.

Get plenty of exercise and rest.

One day to go . . .

Get manicure, pedicure, and other beauty treatments.

Prepare yourself to have fun!

chapter one

First Things First

The big brainstorm! Take note of all the things you simply
must have (or don't want) at your wedding.

Must have	Don't want

● First Things First

Four months to go...
Inform immediate family and close friends of your plans.
Set priorities with groom.
Contact accountants and lawyers, if necessary.
Bookmark relevant Web sites and magazine articles.

You and your fiancé are the ones who have to live with this wedding, so you should be the ones to decide what details are necessary, superfluous, wonderful, overpriced, or just plain silly. If you're culinary connoisseurs, you may want to pay particular attention to the quality of the chardonnay and appetizers. If tradition is deeply valued, then focus your energy on finding the perfect officiant to create the ceremony you want. If you could not care less what the invitations look like, then there's no need to pore over book after book of dainty paper goods. If your one goal in life is to get this whole thing over with, then speed will take precedence over style and substance.

Prioritizing is important in the planning of any wedding, but if you're putting together an instant wedding, it should be item *numero uno* on your agenda. While most wedding books take a chronological approach to organizing a ceremony and reception, your timeline should be determined by what matters most to you. If your heart is set on an haute couture gown, for example, then searching for it will be one of the first things you'll need to do because picking a dress, having it made, and then getting the necessary alterations can take months. Popular wedding sites book up quickly, so if you won't be happy unless you secure a hot locale, then that will dictate your first actions. Other things you can put off indefinitely. Name changes, for example, don't occur until after the wedding, so put off thinking about it for now. Thank-you notes can be ordered alongside invitations, but they can just as easily be ordered after all's said and done.

Because of time constraints, instant weddings do require an unusual degree of flexibility. Out of five must-haves, you may be able to get only three. But this is true of any wedding. In the history of marriage there hasn't been a single nuptial event where someone didn't get his or her feelings hurt, or some key element didn't fall through at the last minute. Rest assured, your day will be no different. Weddings, like marriage and life, are wild, unpredictable rides. The key to wedding-day success is not organization but the ability to step back and take it all in, seeing it as the

High-Speed Connecting

The Internet is both a boon and a bane to brides and grooms. Email is fabulous for coordinating and communicating with family and the wedding party. Online registries mean couples with busy schedules can register for linens and stemware at 2 o'clock in the morning. At the same time, it's very easy to waste precious hours on fruitless searches for everything from bridesmaids' dresses to rehearsal dinner spaces.

Below are some tips for making sure your time online is well spent. More specific advice on everything from how to build a wedding Web site to using email to coordinate plans will be offered in the chapters to come.

• Avoid search engines. Sure, they have tons of listings, but most of those listings were bought and paid for, so they're by no means complete. Plus you'll spend way too many hours sorting through all the information you don't want in search of what you do need.

• If you are going to surf the Web, do get recommendations from friends and family first, so you can be very specific in your online queries. For example, type in "Bonnie's Bridal Boutique" instead of "wedding dresses."

• Do check out your local chamber of commerce's Web site or just give them a ring. Most can provide complete lists of restaurants and hotels with banquet halls, boutiques, and other services you'll need—many of which aren't listed in local wedding guides.

• Avoid locations and vendors that are listed on popular wedding Web sites. They're the first to get booked up. This rule applies to listings in local magazines and wedding guides, too.

• Do use email—or even set up a wedding Web site—to communicate with friends and family about everything from travel plans to clothing and registries. It'll save you time and long-distance fees. See Chapter 7 for step-by-step advice on creating your own online wedding home page 101.

magical, silly, beautiful, powerful, erratic thing it is. A perfect day
is not one in which everything goes according to plan, but one in which
everybody has a smashing good time in spite of what went wrong.

Priorities Workshop

A wedding is a lot like an orchestra—many different elements come
together to make one cohesive event. But just as a symphony might
feature strings more than horns, not all aspects of the wedding are equal
in importance. The following pages are intended to help you determine
what you'll need to focus on in the days, weeks, or months to follow,
and what you can slack on. It's recommended that you and your beau
think about these issues separately and then come together to compare
notes over dinner or, since you're in a hurry, coffee. You might find you
agree on everything. More likely, some discussion and compromise may
need to occur.

Because time is of the essence, you will both need to put a lot
of effort—separately and together—into planning. You will need to
collaborate on the invitation list and the ceremony, for example.
Other responsibilities may be split up. One benefit of setting priorities
separately is that it will give you a good sense of what matters more
to which person. If your fiancé cares deeply about the music, then he
should hire the musicians. If you're more keen on floral arrangements,
then that can be your assignment. If neither of you is in dire need of a
wedding cake, then save planning the dessert for last.

To begin, try to imagine the wedding you've always wanted. How
many people will be there? Is there a huge wedding party? Just a

handful of guests? What type of environment will you have—outdoors or at a hotel or in your folks' backyard? Is it daytime or nighttime? What's the decor like? Are you wearing a traditional gown or something colorful and funky? Is it a sit-down dinner or a champagne brunch? Once you have a clear picture in your head, write it all down, making note of what's missing in your vision. For example, you may not imagine yourself in a limo, meaning special transportation is a low priority. Weddings tend to be heavy on details. Being very specific about what you want will save you time in the search for vendors and locations. A well thought-out plan means that you're also less likely to overlook some important component.

Below is a list of the things you'll need to think about. You and your fiancé may find it helpful to create a worksheet, dividing your wedding into the following sections and taking copious brainstorming notes under each category. When you compare notes, highlight the similarities and negotiate over the differences between each of your wishes.

BUDGET How much do you want to spend? Is it more or less than what you have available? Chapter 2 will include more on this subject, but suffice it to say that a budget tends to be the final arbiter in a lot of decisions, so keep it realistic.

SIZE How many guests do you want at the ceremony and at the reception? Are children welcome? Just family, or are friends included too? Last-minute arrangements may be difficult for faraway guests to make, lowering the number of invitees who will be able make it.

LOCATION Are you going to the chapel or to your favorite park? Do you want to be married close to home, close to relatives, or somewhere faraway and exotic? Indoors or outdoors? Hotel ballroom or backyard? Keep in mind that popular locations have long been booked.

TIME OF DAY This element may have a big impact on what sort of reception you'll have—brunch, dinner, or champagne and cake—which in turn has a lot to do with the size of your budget. If time of day isn't important to either of you, you'll have an easier time getting a location you want.

CEREMONY Will it be traditional, religious, secular, or downright weird? What best expresses *your* personalities and beliefs? If you have a specific officiant in mind, is he or she available on such short notice?

RECEPTION From potlucks to fancy feasts—brides and grooms have done it all. Consider your budget, the time of day, and your own quirky palates, and the logical food choice and party style will emerge.

WEDDING PARTY Will you be having just a witness, thank you very much, or will everyone and their cousin be included? Flower girls and ring bearers? What will your attendants be wearing?

COMMUNICATION How will people learn about your wedding—do you need fancy invites, or will a phone call suffice? Will a wedding Web site be helpful, or does everything need to be written on parchment? Invites are another of those order-well-in-advance items—that is, if you order from a stationery store.

RINGS Do you prefer simple bands that can be purchased at any jewelry shop, or do your lovely fingers require brand names or custom-made? Is there a special ring—perhaps a mother's or grandmother's—that you'd prefer to wear? Or maybe matching tattoos are more your thing. If the budget or the schedule is tight, are you willing to wear a temporary ring and get a fancier one later on?

DRESS Oh yes, the dress! Aside from gorgeous, will it be new, used, rented, or borrowed? Will it be white, ivory, blue, or fire-engine red? Will the fellows don tuxedos or freestyle it in suits or something more casual?

PHOTOGRAPHY There are a surprising number of options here. While most people default to traditional posed wedding photographs, photojournalistic style is growing in popularity. Video? Disposable cameras? Digital? While some people pooh-pooh the importance of photography, unlike the music or food it will be around for many years.

FOOD/CATERING Everything from a potluck to a gourmet sit-down dinner is possible. Do you want to hire a caterer separate from the venue, or would you prefer an all-inclusive package? What type of food do you want? Are there any special dishes you'd like to have served? Will your caterer just be providing the food, or will they be involved in coordinating decorations as well?

ALCOHOL Will it be free-flowing or not at all? Will you limit it to beer, champagne, and wine, or will you cough up the dough for an open bar? Are your friends and family the types to be offended if they're asked to pay for well drinks, or will they accept it as par for the course?

ENTERTAINMENT Live or Memorex? Is it important that a specific band or vocalist play? A surprising number of people have strong feelings for or against wedding DJs. Do you plan to have dancing at your reception or just background music while guests mingle?

CAKE Wedding cakes often need to be ordered well in advance, while gourmet birthday cakes are readily available on short notice. Some brides and grooms are opting for cupcakes or even doughnut towers. This writer served tasty flan at her wedding. What do you want to serve for dessert?

REHEARSAL DINNER This is traditionally paid for by the groom's family, but not every guy's parents are that generous or well-off. Will you have one? Who will pay for it? How big will it be? Can his parents organize it, or will the planning be up to you? Many restaurants have special banquet rooms or will host parties during off-hours. If there's a place you adore, you may want to find out if it's available.

HONEYMOON You may dream of exiting beneath a shower of birdseed and heading straight to the airport. Or that may sound like a big pain in the butt to you. Where do you want to go and when? Will you need to take time off work? Do you want to relax or explore a new place? Is the honeymoon included in the wedding budget or will it be paid for separately?

LEGAL ISSUES Your tax and financial status are going to change. Your country of residence may become different as well. Perhaps you're expecting a baby. One or both of you may change your last name. Plus there's that whole wedding license make-it-official thing to think about. The road to Happily Ever After is strewn with paperwork, so start putting your documents together and make any necessary calls to lawyers and accountants as soon as possible.

MISCELLANEOUS Many doodads have been tacked onto the standard wedding components— limousines, ceremony programs, commemorative place card holders, personalized swizzle sticks, party favors, disposable cameras, groom's cakes, engraved cake cutting and serving sets, plumed pens for the guest book, musical garters, toasting glasses, bridal purses, and so on. This list could go on for pages. Ask yourself, which are must-haves and what can you do without?

Writing It Down

There are a number of ways you can approach the process of recording priorities on paper. You and your fiancé may each want to make a page for every category, list the basic elements, and write next to each: *Very Important, Important, Not Sure, No Big Thing*, or *No Thank You*. Or make three columns—*Must Have, Would Like*, and *Don't Want*—and list items underneath them. These documents, along with the many materials you'll be collecting during your planning, can be stored in a binder for easy reference. Four-by-six-inch index cards are another good route and can be organized along with business cards in a small file or box. You might write the category at the top of the card (*Flowers, Food*, or *Music*), list the related details below (*Bouquets, Sit-down Dinner*, or *DJ*), and rank the importance of each from 1 to 5. For the engineering-minded, a cost-benefit analysis, complete with the pros and cons of each element, could work. A more creative approach might be a brainstorm page, covered with notes, circles, connecting lines, and cute drawings. Each couple has a personal approach to getting organized; use the method that works best for you.

Identifying priorities is not easy. The process forces you to search deep inside and figure out just what it is that you really want, that you really care about. When you make the shocking discovery—and, inevitably, you will—that the person with whom you're about to spend the rest of your life has different ideas than you do about something as important as your wedding, you may be tempted to freak out. Don't. Differences are normal and part of the wonderful process of living life together. The good news is that by setting priorities you and your sweetie will be working things out in advance. As a result, you'll be able to move forward with a focused, united vision rather than winging it. You'll save time, too. Rather than meeting with a caterer and saying, "Um, well, what would you recommend?," you'll be able to provide him or her with very clear ideas about what you want and don't want, and you'll find that everything moves along much faster.

Making Time

Kiss your life good-bye for a few weeks, roll up those sleeves, and get to work! Planning a wedding is no small task, and when time is limited it's bound to get in the way of your usual routine.

Does the person you're marrying have a sexy, exotic accent? That's wonderful for you, but the Immigration and Naturalization Service may not share your enthusiasm for this fabulous foreigner of yours. The application process to make your betrothed a citizen or permanent resident of the United States is difficult and time consuming, and success is not guaranteed.

Rather than going it alone, hire an immigration attorney and plan on including his or her fees in your budget. Consult with the lawyer *as soon as* you decide to get married (if you're not sure where to find one, check with your local chapter of the American Bar Association or a nonprofit organization that specializes in immigration), to make sure there's time to file and process the necessary forms before your wedding. Waiting until the last minute to talk to an attorney and do research can have serious consequences and lead to far greater expenses and stress later on.

Paperwork is key to the immigration and naturalization process. Create a file to hold all your documentation—birth certificates, bank statements, phone records—and any other proof you can find that demonstrates that your romance is the real deal.

For the time being, you may want to avoid taking any trips outside the country. Mix-ups can happen at border crossings and at airports, and once someone is deported, getting that person back into the country can take years. (See Randy and Mizas story, page 126.)

29

One event planner estimates that the average wedding takes about 100 hours to plan. Given that there are only 168 hours in a week and around 50 of those are spent in bed, that doesn't leave time for much else when you are working with a short lead time. She advises that you make a plan at the beginning of each week for what you hope to accomplish. Expect the wedding planning to take up the next six weekends of your life. Throw in some weekdays if the wedding is less than a month away.

If you have fewer than a couple of months before your event, plan to take some time off work for meeting with caterers, ministers, and other professionals. Set aside lunch hours for shopping and doing research. If it's important for you to maintain your social life while putting this whole wedding thing together, try to combine planning activities with socializing: have a champagne brunch with girlfriends and then go hunting for dresses, or indulge in that romantic dinner with your sweetie, but have it at a restaurant you're considering for your rehearsal dinner.

The biggest time suck will be searching for vendors and locations. This is where a wedding planner can come in handy. (You'll learn more about consultants in Chapter 2.) In lieu of hiring someone, use the recommendations of others so you don't have to check everyone out yourself. If you recently attended a wedding that you really liked, find out who catered it, who did the flowers, and so on. Don't feel guilty if you have to rely on your network of friends and family to help you with some of the planning. Put willing members of your wedding party, your mom, and your future father-in-law to work making calls to florists, liquor stores, and party rental suppliers.

Finally, while it may sound absurd, don't drive yourself completely insane. Take time off to care for your mental and physical health. While the wedding is your focus, make sure to leave some time for other activities. If you find yourself feeling grouchy or your libido begins to fade into oblivion, step back, take a deep breath, and figure out how you can save some time and energy.

chapter two
The Damage

Where will the money come from? Calculate your assets
and liabilities in this handy space.

....
....
....
....
....
....
....
....
....
....
....
....
....
....
....
....
....
....
....
....
....
....
....

❀ The Damage

35

Four months to go...	
Evaluate your finances.	
Set a realistic budget.	
Ask for money, if needed.	
Create a style for the reception.	
Hire a wedding coordinator.	

Bad news first. According to recent figures, the average wedding costs around $20,000. (Feel free to put this book down and belt out a few primal screams, if need be.) That number can go up if you happen to live in a well-heeled urban metropolis, or it may go down if you live in a rural area. Now, that's a lot of dough for anyone to cough up at once and, because your wedding is last minute, you probably haven't spent the last year scrimping and saving for the big event.

It gets worse. The wedding industrial complex is not your friend. In fact, it's well known that everyone from caterers and florists to hotels and limo companies jack up their prices when it comes to weddings. So while they're smiling and saying sweet things like "Congratulations!" and "You're going to have the day you've always dreamed of," in truth they're laughing all the way to the bank. They figure that it's the biggest day of your life thus far, so you'll find a way to pay. Sadly, they're usually right.

And—one last bit of bad news—this wedding industry does not look kindly upon last-minute arrangements. More precisely, they penalize you for them. Rush orders for things like invitations, dresses, and airfare (to name a few) come at a premium, so be prepared to cough up a little more than the average for these things or find a way to work with vendors that don't specialize in nuptials. For example, hotels and restaurants that usually cater to businesses are used to hosting last-minute parties and events.

Finally, some good news. Plenty of couples find ways to cut down the cost of their weddings without sacrificing good taste or their personal style. There is no need to spend $20,000 if you can't afford it.

And there's no reason not to spend $100,000 if you can afford it and that's what you really want to do.

Budgeting

If your parents are footing the bill, then congratulations. These days, many families will help out, but much of the financial burden is the bride and groom's to bear. If it's a second wedding or your family simply doesn't have the means to assist, then you may be paying for the whole shebang. Regardless of how you finance your event, you're going to need to start with a budget.

There will be times when a budget feels like your worst enemy, like when you want a string quartet but the budget only leaves room for one student violinist. Remember: the budget is your friend. Sticking to a good budget will keep costs from spiraling out of control. A budget will help you eliminate frivolous options, saving valuable time. A budget can help you ensure that there's money left over after the wedding for buying a house, having a child, or taking a long and restful honeymoon.

As you're fretting over pricey orchids versus playful mums or a full bar versus beer and wine, it'll be helpful to keep in mind that the money must come from *somewhere*. You may think you have to have a sit-down dinner, until you realize that it means draining your retirement account. So ask yourself —and be honest when you answer—*Where will the money come from?* Taking out a loan means starting your marriage in debt, which may hinder attempts to get a mortgage or cause unnecessary stress. Borrowing from parents may lead to hard feelings when payment comes due. Using your savings means it won't be there for emergencies. Older newlyweds may prefer a modest wedding in order to keep their retirement funds intact.

At the same time, it's your wedding. It doesn't happen very often, so it's OK to treat it like the special event it is. You may be nowhere near settling down with a big mortgage and a little whippersnapper, so a big party can be easily justified. There's nothing wrong with going a little over the top for what is a once-in-a-lifetime (OK, maybe twice) event. The trick is to take each decision seriously no matter how quickly it must be made, weigh all the options, and avoid headaches later.

Sit down with your fiancé (and parents, if they'll be contributing). Decide just how much you have to spend. Figure out where the money will come from and how it will impact your overall budget and lifestyle.

Is it worth it to forgo manicures and organic produce for several months in order to have a kickin' band play at your reception? Then go for it! Would you be more comfortable dipping into your savings account than taking out a wedding loan? Let your intentions be known. Talking honestly about money from the start will save you from numerous misunderstandings in the future.

Don't fret if your budget is tiny. Plenty of couples have had splendid, memorable nuptials on very little money. Spending less cash means you'll have to be more creative, which is never a bad thing when it comes to a wedding.

WHERE DOES THE MONEY COME FROM? Now, clear off the kitchen table! Dust off those bank statements! Get out the calculator! Call the accountant! It is time to do some math. Figure out how much you have, how much you can spend, and how you want to spend it, based on your priorities.

Here are some obvious and not-so-obvious places where funding for your event may be lurking:

• Savings accounts

• Retirement plans: If you borrow from yourself, the interest gets paid back to you.

• Loans from parents or close friends

• Credit cards or loans (Note: Special wedding loans that are advertised in bridal magazines often have outrageously high interest rates. Look elsewhere before you succumb to these tempting offers.)

• Sale of assets like property, stock, or a second car

• Bonus checks or unexpected windfall; inheritance

• Unclaimed tax refunds

• Garage sales: Unload some junk before the wedding booty starts flowing in!

• Gifts: Depending on how formal or casual your family is, it may be acceptable to ask for money instead of presents, but don't be upset if people still opt for the latter.

From "Will you?" to "I do!" in twenty-four hours? As crazy as it sounds, it can be done! Jolayne Marsh and Christopher Madden, neighbors in British Columbia, had been feverishly dating for seven whole weeks when one day, quite coincidentally, each gave the other a note that brought up the *M* word.

They stayed up all night talking about it. When the sun rose, they marched over to the licensing office, coughed up the $75 fee, bought a pair of cheap silver rings, and dropped in on a neighbor who was a justice of the peace. She agreed to perform the ceremony once she'd fully woken up from her nap.

Jolayne dashed home and threw on a favorite dress. Christopher donned a suit. They bought a bouquet of orchids from a nearby florist and called two unemployed friends, who were available to be witnesses on a weekday. Forty minutes later, the impromptu wedding party headed to the neighbor's house for a simple civil ceremony. That night, the newlyweds went out to dinner with a few stunned friends. Wedding and reception cost around $200, including the rings.

"It was really romantic," Jolayne recalls. "We both really wanted to build our own family from scratch. When we decided to make it official, we wanted people to treat us like family immediately."

Of course, telling their folks wasn't easy, but Jolayne assures us that they took it pretty well considering neither set of parents had even met their child's new spouse. The next day, Jolayne's dad took them out to lunch. "Dad was excited that we did it so rashly," Jolayne explains. Later on, Christopher's family threw a reception for them.

Although Jolayne sometimes wishes they had done something more inclusive—a big bash for their friends, perhaps—she says, "We loved doing it. We love the story. It wasn't a mistake." She's also glad that the wedding was done completely on their terms. "We didn't have people we didn't want hanging around . . . One of the other benefits is there was none of that cold-feet period. We jumped in headfirst."

Two months later, the newlyweds finally got around to moving in together.

What Are Wedding Planners Good for, Anyway?

In situations where time is less plentiful than money, a wedding planner can be a real lifesaver. The wedding planner or consultant knows which vendors are good to work with and whether they're within your budget, and he or she can quickly find out if they're available on your day. That saves you countless frustrating searches and hours of tedious cold-calling. If your wedding will take place far from where you live, utilizing a consultant's knowledge and skills may be a necessity.

However, good help doesn't come cheap. Expect to tack on an additional 10 to 15 percent to your total wedding bill for the full services of a planner. If that's too high for you, look for consultants who offer their services on a limited basis, so you can benefit from their expertise without breaking the bank. For an hourly fee consultants can meet with you for a productive planning session or show up on the day of your wedding to make sure that everything goes smoothly.

If you decide to use a consultant, find someone whom both of you trust and like. Make sure their office is well kept and their stationery is professional. Get references and ask for evidence of completed seminars and courses. While you will rely on this person's extensive knowledge of wedding venues, caterers, florists, and invitation printers, a consultant's job is *not* to tell you how to organize your wedding. His or her job is to make your ideas happen within your budget, so watch out for someone who contradicts you or insists on a "right" way of doing things. A wedding planner who doesn't give you undivided attention during consultation meetings certainly shouldn't be trusted with your wedding. And if a consultant insists that you sit through two boring hours of his or her personal wedding video, run far, far away. (Yes, that really happened to someone.)

The best way to start looking for a consultant (other than getting recommendations from friends and family) is to contact a wedding planners organization. Members must meet certain standards to join, so you can be certain that the first level of screening has been covered. For associations and their contact information, see the Resources section, page 142. Your search will be more difficult if your wedding's in June or July, when most consultants are booked to the gills with events.

Remember, even the best of business relationships can turn sour, so make sure to include a clause in your contract that gives you sufficient time to get out of it. The clause might read something like this: "If the Couple or Wedding Planner wishes to cancel this contract for any reason, they must do so at least 30 (thirty) days before the event. If the Couple or Wedding Planner cancels 30 (thirty) days or more before the event, the Couple will receive a full refund of their deposit, minus a $35-per-hour fee for work completed. If the Wedding Planner cancels less than 30 (thirty) days before the event, he or she will provide the Couple with a replacement wedding planner under the same terms and conditions at no additional cost."

41

Questions to Ask a Potential Wedding Planner

• Are you available on our chosen date?

• Have you ever planned a wedding on short notice? What did you do?

• How many other weddings will you be handling on or around our date?

• How long have you been working as a wedding consultant?

• Why did you become a wedding consultant?

• How many weddings have you planned? How many do you plan, on average, per year? (Be sure to ask to see pictures and for several references.)

• Are you a member of any professional organizations?

• Do you have a business license?

• Do you receive commissions from any vendors? (If the answer is yes, steer clear. This wedding planner is paid to direct you toward certain businesses, regardless of what's in your best interest.)

• What are your fees and how does your billing system work?

• What do we get in return for our money?

• Can you work within our budget?

• How many hours per week are you available to spend consulting with us on this event?

• How often do you provide updates to your clients and how are they communicated (by phone, email, or fax)?

• How will you dress on the day of the event?

• What would you consider the strangest request you've ever received from a client?

• Has anyone asked you to do something for their wedding that you felt was improper? What was it, and how did you handle it?

• Will we be penalized if we decide not to work with you after the contract is signed?

• Will you guarantee backup arrangements if you suddenly become sick or otherwise unavailable on our wedding day?

Money can be one of the most stressful aspects of a wedding—especially when there isn't much of it around. Happily, a fairy-tale wedding needn't cost a million bucks. It needn't even *look* like it cost a million bucks. The red-carpet treatment simply isn't worth getting in over your heads budgetwise. At the same time, if you can afford to spend a little extra, spend it on time-savers, like a wedding planner and rush orders. In short, be realistic and be wise. Cinderella did big things with little more than a pumpkin and a borrowed dress, and so can you!

chapter three
Where?! When?!

Shortlisted! A handy spot to write down the names and numbers of your top wedding location picks.

....
....
....
....
....
....
....
....
....
....
....
....
....
....
....
....
....
....
....
....
....

❀ Where?! When?!

Four months to go...

Finalize the guest list; check spelling and addresses.

Visit and book reception and ceremony locations.

Three months to go...

Communicate key details to family, wedding party, and far-flung guests.

Delegate key tasks to family and wedding party.

Of all the planning you'll be doing over the next few weeks, picking a place will be among the most challenging—though also important and exciting—tasks you accomplish. Not only are the most popular sites often booked up a year or more in advance, but finding a location also requires a great deal of legwork. You'll probably need to make a ton of phone calls, take time out to visit places, talk to event planners, and attend tastings with on-site caterers. It's for this reason that most wedding guides advise that you book your site at least a year in advance. And without exception the best and most popular places fill up fast. This means that you will have to be more creative than most couples. You'll have to search in unconventional places and, in some cases, use your creativity and imagination to make up for things your site may be lacking. Since you don't have a year, you should make picking a location your first job after your priorities are set and budgets are organized. The good news is that once you've picked a spot a lot of other aspects will automatically fall into place.

Obviously, there are a ton of considerations when it comes to deciding where to have your wedding. Having those priorities in hand will help you hone in on your options. Is a dramatic, natural setting important to you? Then you'll probably want to cross off places that are indoors or don't have views. If having your whole, huge family present is a top desire, then you'll need to look for a space that's big enough to accommodate them. A wedding at your parents' home may be easy on relatives, but it may be difficult for your newer friends if you grew up far from your present hometown. Getting married at a beach means you'll have to rent a tent, tables, chairs, stemware, and so on, plus find a caterer who's willing and able to serve food there. An all-inclusive hotel package may be easy, but if the food and decor don't sufficiently express your personalities, you may find yourself putting in extra effort on the decorating front.

Because you're booking things late in the game, you'll probably need to be a little flexible about things that are less important to you. For example, if it's essential to you to exchange vows in a church or if you absolutely must hold your reception at your grandparents' country club, you may need to accept an unconventional time slot—a weekday, for example, or a morning—to make it work.

Oh, Baby!

Are you pregnant? If you're in your first trimester, you may want to get a good sense of how you're feeling throughout the day before picking a time for your event. The last thing you want is to feel like Linda Blair as you make your way down the aisle! Some women really do get *morning* sickness, but for others it can strike in the afternoon or at night. Later in the pregnancy, you may get more tired at certain times of the day. And consider your location: an outdoor setting may be affordable and lovely, but it doesn't necessarily offer many places for the mom-to-be to sit and rest. Pay attention to what your body is telling you and plan accordingly. Also, talk to your doctor. If it's a high-risk pregnancy, the stress of a wedding may be too much for you to take right now.

On the opposite side of the coin, will you be menstruating? If your period tends to be irregular, it may be difficult for you to plan around it. But for everyone else, calculating just when you'll be bleeding (not to mention bloating, PMSing, having mood swings, and cramping) will be worth your while when setting a date. There are a number of online menstrual calculators to make this process mindlessly easy, although going the old-fashioned calendar-and-a-pen route works just as well. (See Resources at the end of this book.)

Keep in mind that it's not one location you are selecting and paying for, it's three: venues for the rehearsal dinner, ceremony, *and* reception. You may be in luck, though: the funky bistro that's a bit too hip for the reception may be ideal for the rehearsal dinner or a wedding shower, so file away good places, even if you think they are unusable. They may come in handy later.

The Guest List

An important step in picking a place is to create a rough guest list. You don't have to decide exactly whom you're going to invite right this instant, but you definitely can't determine where you can hold your event until you have an idea of how many folks the place will need to accommodate.

The guest list can be a surprisingly telling piece of paper, and people make up all sorts of rules about who does and doesn't get invited. Some say no kids, flat out; others say only immediate family. One couple may only invite people they see on a weekly basis, while others won't feel right unless every twice-removed cousin feels welcome. When parents are footing the bill, they may rightly insist on including some of their old friends, while some brides and grooms may want to invite people representative of various periods and aspects of their lives—his quirky college roommate, your cubicle mate from work, and long-lost "crazy" Uncle Bob. If you're having a destination wedding, inviting just a handful of friends and close relatives is more than sufficient. Go with your gut. Obviously, your budget will have a huge impact as well; you may want to invite a ton of people but only be able to afford dinner for fifty, for example.

If you and your intended disagree on who's worthy and who's not, some quick compromising and bargaining may be necessary. In that case, compensate (don't invite kids but do provide childcare nearby), swap (his scary aunt Gertrude gets to come if your outrageous gal pal whom he despises is invited, too), and place limits (exes aren't allowed, unless they're currently friends with both of you).

As with setting priorities, it's easiest for bride and groom to make separate lists of the people each would like to be there, and then put the lists together, talk about them over a soothing bottle of wine, and whittle the number down as needed.

Once you've picked your date and location, you can firm up the invitation list. A spreadsheet is perfect for something like this, because it can hold not only names and addresses but also spaces to write down whether an R.S.V.P. was received, gifts, and even table assignments. Be sure to check the spelling of names and updated addresses. One advantage of getting married close to the holidays is that most holiday cards you receive will include a recent return address.

Where to Look

Once you have a sense of the number of guests, you can start looking for a location. The venues listed in bridal guides are most likely to be taken, although that's not necessarily a given. People do cancel. Prime Saturdays are sometimes mysteriously skipped over. If there's somewhere you have in mind, but you think it's not likely to be available, pick up the phone anyway! You may be surprised at what a little sweet-talking and finagling can get you. Perhaps the main ballroom is booked, but a lovely suite is open. Your favorite restaurant might be full but able to cater an event that's held elsewhere. You won't know until you try.

Fortunately there are many great alternatives and effective techniques for betrothed couples to find a place in a hurry. Here are a few suggestions to help get your creative juices flowing:

EMBRACE MONDAY THROUGH FRIDAY Is there a spot you've always dreamed of for your wedding? Don't despair if it's booked every weekend until 2040. Call up the place and ask in your sweetest voice if there's an opening on a weekday or weeknight. Friends and family worth their salt won't mind taking a day or two off for your wedding.

BREAK IT UP If your ceremony spot is only available in the morning and your reception venue of choice can only make room for you in the evening, consider splitting the events up. Invite close friends and relatives to an intimate morning ceremony followed by a fabulous bash that evening. Everyone gets to take a nap, and you get to spend a luxurious long day alone with your now-husband before putting on your party dress. What's not to love?

AH, THE GREAT OUTDOORS Your local parks and recreation department likely has numerous facilities available to be rented for events—both indoors and out. Beaches and public parks may require permits for certain types of gatherings, but generally they are free, spacious, and mighty beautiful. Urbanites might want to consult with friends who live or work in skyscrapers; often there are rooftop facilities in offices or apartment buildings that provide stunning views at little cost.

HOME, SWEET HOME A home-based wedding can be simultaneously elegant and cozy, and as extravagant or casual as you desire. A friend's lush rose garden may be just as nice as a hotel courtyard, and who can beat a mom's hospitality? Friends who live in a condominium complex may be able to hook you up with their on-site clubhouse or swimming pool.

CITY HALL Before weddings were elevated to the level of myth and fairy tale, they were often practical, small-scale events that would start at the local city hall. In many ways, the simple civil ceremony is one of the most traditional options around, and the grand historical architecture may provide a dramatic setting for your exchange of vows.

FAR, FAR AWAY One way to prevent hurt feelings caused by a limited guest list or last-minute elopement is to take your wedding overseas. What could be more romantic than riding through a Greek village on donkeys while the locals applaud, or saying "I do" in front of a dramatic tropical waterfall? Wedding travel packages can be found for destinations from Hawaii to Moscow and everywhere in between and are perfect for just the two of you, or a small group of immediate family and close friends.

THE CHAPEL OF LOVE If religion is a big part of your life, or if you just love the theatrics of a traditional religious ceremony, then it's likely you'll want to be wed in a church, synagogue, or mosque. Do you or your parents belong to a religious congregation or parish? Often these places set aside wedding time slots just for members. Again, you'll have to contend with the fact that most Saturdays are booked in advance. If this is the case, see if there's not a neighboring church that's available or ask for a weekday or weeknight instead. Many facilities include kitchens and banquet halls where you can celebrate after the ceremony.

MEMORY LANE Couples rarely meet in a place as romantic as the one where they eventually get married, but that doesn't mean the place where eyes first locked, hands first touched, or saliva was first exchanged isn't special. Marrying in the bar where you first bumped into each other or at the dog park where your pups introduced the two of you can be very meaningful, not to mention fun. If it's a public place, make sure to check with the city for restrictions and permits.

UNLIKELY LOCALES Your local nursery may have never hosted a wedding, but that doesn't mean the owners won't be willing to, if you ask nicely. Galleries, schools, and clubs can all provide excellent backdrops for your event. In cities, interior decorators often doll up unoccupied houses as showcases for their work, which can then be rented out for events. Lavish private mansions are often maintained by holding events like weddings and bat mitzvahs. Often they advertise only by word of mouth, so be sure to ask around.

PACKAGES Many hotels and popular destinations like Hawaii and Las Vegas offer all-inclusive wedding packages. For the couple that's short on time and not terribly picky, it can be a wonderful time-saver to get your flowers, cake, food, officiant, even music all from the same place. Personal touches can be added to things like favors or clothing.

RESTAURANTS If your wedding is going to be on the smaller side, a nice restaurant can be a perfect setting for your reception (and even ceremony). If the establishment doesn't have a private room or courtyard, plan your party for hours when the restaurant is usually closed, so you don't have to pay a staggering buy-out fee (which basically covers what they would be making if regular customers were there). Check with your local chamber of commerce and visitor's bureau for lists of restaurants that are available for special events.

Las Vegas is the Instant Wedding capital of the world. Where else can you show up without notice or blood test, at any hour of the day or night, hand over fifty bucks, and get hitched before a minister in an Elvis suit? Not many places, which is why Clark County, Nevada, issues a whopping one hundred twenty thousand marriage licenses per year.

Aside from making marriage as convenient and affordable as fast food, Las Vegas does kitsch like nowhere else. Brides and grooms who eschew sentimentality for humor and self-expression can have themselves an Elvis, Star Trek, nude, goth, Dracula, pirate, bungee-jumping, mafia, horseback, or even cowboy-style shotgun wedding (complete with an angry father, played by an actor), should they so desire. There's even a replica of the Sistine Chapel painted by a descendant of the master himself available for last-minute nuptials. A popular tourist destination, Las Vegas offers cheap airfares, food, and accommodations—plus plenty of entertainment—to visiting guests.

Few know the ins and outs of the Las Vegas wedding scene better than Vicki Marinich. Once named Las Vegas's top wedding planner, she's provided hundreds of couples with low-cost, last-minute weddings for more than five years. So it

makes sense that her own wedding, to John Marinich, her partner of over eight years, would be about as Vegas as they come.

It all started two weeks before Valentine's Day, when the host of a local morning TV show called her for help with a segment they were airing. "They said they would be filming four Valentine's Day weddings in Las Vegas," Vicki recalls. "They were going to pay for the formal wear, [facility] rental, the wedding cake, the flowers, and a small appetizer reception. So I told John, 'I think this is a sign.' We became bride and groom and it was stunning!"

Vicki and John got married in the Wedding Mobile, a lushly decorated coach complete with disco lights, a small dance floor, and room for twenty guests. With four television crew members, the show's host, Vicki's daughter, and the minister present, Vicki and John were married as they drove down Las Vegas's famous neon-lit Strip.

"The views of the hotels were stunning. The fountains at Bellagio were going off when we passed. The tourists could easily see the celebration going on inside," she recalls fondly. "We were waving out all of the windows to the tourists as we traveled and celebrated. It was really quite fabulous!"

54

Visiting Tips

Unless you know a site really, really well, you'll probably want to visit it before committing. To save time, be fairly certain you are interested in a place before even making an appointment to stop by. Do your research and call with any outstanding questions *before* scheduling a visit. Be sure to have your list of must-haves and must-not-haves handy as you talk to the location's facilitator. Don't like what you see? It's OK to say, "Thanks, but this isn't quite what we had in mind," and then go on your merry way.

Questions to Ask Before Visiting a Facility

• What's the total fee for the facility and what does that include?

• What are the time limits? Do we have just four hours or all day? What's the penalty for going overtime?

• Are there other events scheduled for the space on our chosen day (meaning you'll have to push people out when it's over or rush to get everything ready)?

• Are there other events going on elsewhere in the facility? (The last thing you need is to discover that you'll be sharing a lobby and bathrooms with the National Swingers Association.)

• Are we required to go with a certain caterer or can we choose our own? Can we bring our own alcohol?

• Who is responsible for cleanup? Is cleanup included in the total amount of time?

• Are tables, chairs, linens, flatware, and glasses included, or will we have to rent them?

• Is there sufficient parking? How many spaces? Are they paid or free?

• If the wedding's taking place outdoors, do you offer an indoor alternative in case of bad weather?

- How many restrooms are there? Where are they located?

- Will a staff member from the facility be on hand to assist us on the day of the event?

- Can we get married and have our reception in the same place, or will separate locations (and fees) be necessary?

- Are the facilities set up to accommodate elderly people and those in wheelchairs?

- Are packages available or will we be making most of the arrangements (food, alcohol, service, and so on) ourselves?

- Are hotel accommodations available on the premises? Are discounts at the venue or with a partner hotel available?

- Is the site insured in case of an accident?

- Will we need to purchase additional permits for things like amplified music, heat lamps, and alcohol?

- What is the cancellation policy?

Once you've locked in on a place, there are several more things to think about before plunking down a deposit and signing the contract. First off, time of day! If you're having a sunset wedding, be sure to swing by *at sunset*. That way you can compare what your place will actually look like with the vision in your mind. Then there's the weather. While it's impossible to absolutely predict what the conditions will be, looking at a weather almanac (there are plenty online) to ascertain the norm will give you a better sense of whether you'll need to prepare for rain or pack some sunscreen. Finally, if possible, drop in on another event that's being held at your space. It's a great way to spot potential problems, get ideas, and begin thinking about what will and won't work in your venue.

Gay Vermont

On July 1, 2000, the state of Vermont, in the northeastern United States, became one of the few places on Earth to confer the legal benefits of marriage to same-sex couples, and the gay wedding industry has been booming there ever since. For gay couples who wish to make things really, truly official, Vermont is the place to go (although your Civil Union won't be officially recognized in most other places). A Vermont Civil Union license costs a mere $20, can be obtained just a day in advance, and can be signed by a judge, justice of the peace, or minister. Other states, like California, have domestic partner- ship laws that enable gay couples to enjoy some, but not all, of the same rights as those of heterosexual married couples.

Lack of legal status has not stopped many gay couples from exchanging vows and rings before friends and family members, of course. While the law may not endorse these unions, for those involved, the com- mitment is as strong and the cere- mony as meaningful as those of a legally sanctioned wedding. For information on Vermont weddings, gay wedding planners, and gay- friendly honeymoon destinations, see the Resources section at the end of this book.

Communicating Your Plans

Chapter 7 will delve into invitations and other communications more deeply. For now, though, suffice it to say that your hastily planned wedding will probably take quite a few folks by surprise. Communication is an important element in any wedding; when you're asking people to make last-minute plans, it becomes crucial.

As soon as you know that you're getting married in a hurry, be kind enough to inform those whose lives will be most affected by it—mom, dad, grandma, your best friends, the person whose backyard you hope to use, and your hairdresser. Presumably you'll want to let those in your closest circle know in person, although in a pinch a phone call or email may be fine. Once you have a place and a date nailed down, tell the people on your invitation list what's happening right away. Email is the fastest way to distribute news in bulk quantities. If your family has a phone tree established, make the needed calls and let gossip do the rest of the work. Spreading the word will allow your guests to resolve any conflicting plans and make travel arrangements, while buying you time before you need to work on the invitations. ("Save the date" cards, another great way to inform guests in advance, will be discussed at length in Chapter 7.)

Once you and your fiancé have picked a place, you'll be amazed at how many other things fall into place. If you can, visit your location several times before your actual event, in order to get familiar with its layout and nuances. Go on site to discuss details with caterers and florists and to pick out picture-perfect spots with your photographer. If there are other weddings scheduled to take place at your spot, see if you can peek in on them to get ideas for decorating and room arrangements. Remember that even the dullest of spots will be magically transformed when filled with people you love and all those happy vibes.

Thanks, But No Thanks

You'll find as you communicate your exciting news that many people will offer to help out, and you should definitely take advantage of that. One of the benefits of giving people as much advance warning as possible is that they can then set aside the time to assist you. At the same time, don't feel obligated to take people up on their offer. Your best friend may be a wonderful person but a total flake—definitely not someone you'd want to trust with scheduling your wedding-day beauty treatments. Your aunt Gilda may have the best intentions when she offers to design your floral arrangements, but if you know that her arrangement skills are lacking, her roses are wilting, or her taste is less than stylish, then say, "Thank you very much, but we already have something else lined up."

chapter four
Speedy Ceremonies

More than "I do." Here's a place to write down special songs, rituals,
and other fun stuff that you want to be part of your ceremony.

❀ Speedy Ceremonies

Four months to go...
Pick a venue, if different from reception.
Three months to go...
Choose an officiant and witness.
Two months to go...
Pick out and order flowers and decorations.
One month to go...
Get marriage license and blood tests (if required).
Choose or write a ceremony script.
One week to go...
Review final ceremony script and details with officiant.

Although some couples prefer to dispense with the procession and speed through the vows, for most, a marriage ceremony of some kind will very likely be an important part of the wedding day. Fortunately, it is one of the easiest and quickest things to put together. You need just a few basic things: find a place to do the deed, an officiant, a witness, and a marriage license, and you're set! Other things—music, original vows, flowers, bridesmaids, and aisle runners—are nice but not at all necessary. So unless you're planning a grand theatrical production complete with interpretive dancers, laser show, and an Austrian boys choir, you don't have to worry about planning the ceremony right away. Phew.

With that said, *some* arrangements shouldn't be left off until the eleventh hour either. Ministers and churches need to be booked in advance and, like most wedding vendors, get booked up early during popular times and seasons. If these are high priorities for you, then you may want to start planning the ceremony sooner. Because some states

It's natural to want your close friends and siblings to feel included, but when time is of the essence, having a wedding party may be more trouble than it's worth. You'll be responsible for choosing their outfits, which means more time spent shopping. If they're coming from out of town, they may look to you for help finding accommodations. Without a wedding party, you may even be able to skip the rehearsal dinner. No bridesmaids or groomsmen also means no gifts to be bought. You can still ask close friends and siblings to act as attendants on the day of the wedding, making sure you have everything you need and nothing you don't.

64   have mandatory waiting periods before you can get legally hitched and items like birth certificates sometimes need to be unearthed or ordered, checking with your county courthouse to find out what's required of you is also a good thing to do early.

Picking the Spot

In Chapter 3 we discussed finding a location for both the wedding and the reception, but what if you're still looking for the right spot for just your ceremony? There are many ideal places to get married—a glorious bluff overlooking the sea, your grandma's rose garden, the local chapel, a drive-through window in Las Vegas—depending on what you and your groom want. Exchanging vows before a grand landscape can evoke a sweeping narrative of love and destiny, while a more intimate setting may reinforce the bonds of family and friendship that keep a relationship strong. A church sets a spiritual tone, obviously, while a wooded setting celebrates more earthbound values.

One of the easiest things you can do is exchange vows at the place where your reception will happen. After all, you've gone to the trouble

When Julie Chiron, a Web entrepreneur, and Craig Gordan, an attorney, decided to get married, they had a pretty strong vision of what their ceremony would be like. They wanted an event that would be for just the two of them, in a location neither of them had been to (so there wouldn't be any previous history or memories), and they wanted to incorporate nature as well as some sacred rituals from other cultures into their event.

It was February when they picked a national park in California with a nice lodge. They chose the last week of April, because prices were set to go up in May. The plan was to take a three-mile circular hike in full wedding regalia, with stops along the way for the various rituals they had incorporated—including a Huichol Prayer Arrow Ceremony, the reading and burning of special blessings written by friends and family, as well as an exchange of vows and rings.

On the day they arrived, a huge snowstorm blew into town. By the second day at the lodge it was clear they'd have to switch to Plan B. Frustrated but determined, the couple packed up their things and drove to the coast for warmer climes, stopping at various beaches to perform their rituals as planned.

"We did the things we wanted to on the beaches, but it was a different experience. As a couple we had to deal with adversity and plans falling through. Luckily we didn't have to move 150 people with us," Julie recalls.

All in all, Julie says, it was a beautiful day. The couple took their time as they made their way down the coast, documenting the events of the whole day with the help of cameras placed on tripods. Back in their hometown several days later, they stopped at the courthouse to make it official. They didn't bring a witness, but the passing bike messenger they recruited gladly signed the papers and snapped a few photos after making his delivery.

Julie and Craig decided to throw a big party for family and friends in September of that year. "It took a lot of the pressure off," Julie says. "We'd already taken care of ourselves, already made our commitments, got our rings, and everything. All that remained was just a fun day; it was more like a family reunion than anything."

65

of finding and booking the place. Why not make the most of it? If you're outside, set up some chairs or picnic blankets for your guests. If the ceremony is short and the guest list is small, you may want to consider having guests stand in a circle around you (but be sure that elderly guests have seats and plenty of shade). Indoors or outdoors, you can push tables to the side for the ceremony if need be, then replace them for the reception.

Churches, like reception spots, are often booked well in advance, so having your wedding during off-hours will certainly help you secure a preferred house of worship. For example, if your local chapel has another wedding booked on Saturday afternoon, consider Saturday morning. Remember, while it may be a little awkward, there's nothing wrong with having a wedding early in the day and the reception later that evening. Maybe the ceremony will be a small affair, limited to family and close friends, while the reception will be open to a larger guest list. The more flexible you are, the easier it will be to make what you want work within your schedule.

For destination and package weddings, the ceremony spot and officiant are usually part of the deal—a Grand Canyon cliff or dramatic Maui waterfall are typical choices. Ditto if you're going to Las Vegas, where the glowing neon of the Strip or a kitschy chapel altar will set a playful tone. Many city halls perform weddings below spacious rotundas or in old-fashioned, musty offices with tall windows and antique books, rooting your ceremony in tradition and civic pride. For ceremonies of these kinds, all you really need to do is show up and say "I do." If you want to throw something personal into the mix, such as original vows or a special song, you'll need to let the place know ahead of time.

Making It Official

Rings and vows are lovely, but it's paperwork that makes your marriage official, allowing your spouse to share health benefits while you're living and oversee your affairs when you die (hopefully many decades from now). Contact your county offices as soon as possible to find out the requirements for a marriage license. Some states require blood tests and

Most wedding ceremonies begin with a processional and end with a recessional. Usually accompanied by music, these dramatic choreographed entrances and exits are one of the most exciting, emotional moments of the day.

The bride's and groom's religious affiliations tend to dictate who's included in the processional and recessional and the order in which they will walk. In Jewish ceremonies, the rabbi leads the processional, which includes grandparents, groomsmen, the groom accompanied by his parents, bridesmaids, the bride, and her parents, whereas in a Christian wedding, the groom, groomsmen, and minister or priest wait at the altar while the bridesmaids and the bride, accompanied by her father, walk in the processional. In a Jewish ceremony, the groom's side is on the left and the bride's side is on the right, and in a Christian one, it's reversed. These are just two examples! Every religious and cultural tradition has its own unique take.

If you're concerned about doing things the proper way, you'll want to consult a book on religious traditions or ask your officiant. Plenty of couples have combined traditions, while others have come up with their own processional and recessional styles.

waiting periods, while in other places you can show up, get licensed, and get hitched all in a matter of minutes. Knowing in advance what's required of you will enable you to gather the necessary paperwork (birth certificates, photo IDs, medical records), saving you last-minute stress.

Once you have the license, it will need to be signed by an officiant. If you're having a civil ceremony, there will be a judge or justice of the peace on hand at the county courthouse to provide the signature that seals the deal. A licensed minister, rabbi, notary, mayor, magistrate, or clerk may also do. You will also need to obtain the John Hancock of a witness (often a parent or someone from your wedding party).

And then there's the Universal Life Church route. Founded in the late 1950s and headquartered in Modesto, California, ULC has been providing free and easy ordination to everyone from '60s peaceniks who used the title of minister to evade the draft to ordinary folks who have wished to perform wedding ceremonies. They even sell wedding-ceremony kits through their Web site. Thanks to this organization, you can forgo the priest or judge and have a close family friend, a mentor, your Uncle Bob, your Aunt Suzie, or your great pal with the fabulous speaking voice perform your ceremony and sign the papers. Ordination is free and completely official, and it can be done over the Internet in less than three minutes. There are also links to wedding ceremony scripts and other helpful information on the ULC Web site. (See the Resources section at the end of this book.)

The Wedding Script

Brides and grooms now have unprecedented freedom when it comes to the wedding ceremony, and indeed the trend has been to make the ritual something that truly reflects the individuals involved. Today couples can work with a preexisting script, write their own, or do a little bit of both—using music, storytelling, costume, and other elements to make their event truly unique.

Religious and civic ceremonies tend to follow a set script. There are also numerous books and Web sites available detailing traditional and unusual ceremonies from a vast number of countries and religions— Islam, Catholicism, Hinduism, and Wicca, to name a few. Following a preexisting script is truly the easiest and fastest route to go, and it can be a real lifesaver if you're not exactly Shakespeare. Alas, these ceremonies aren't exactly personal, either, which is why, if you go this route, you may wish to spice things up with musical interludes or carefully selected readings.

More and more couples are choosing to write their wedding ceremonies, or at least their vows, from scratch. Often cultural and religious traditions, such as the breaking of the glass in a Jewish ceremony or lighting of a unity candle (of European origin), are woven into the program. For example, getting married beneath a canopy is a part of many religious ceremonies, including Jewish and Hindu, and is a nice way of drawing focus to the bride and groom. In Quaker ceremonies, guests may rise and contribute stories, songs, prayers, or blessings as they are so moved, and the marriage certificate, usually a large piece of parchment adorned by a calligrapher, is signed by all in attendance. Having someone tell the story of how you and your groom met and fell in love makes a wonderful centerpiece for a wedding ceremony; it can be especially helpful because many of your guests may be foggy on the details of your courtship. Truly the options are limitless, and your choices will reflect your individuality.

Decor, music, and other extras will only add to the originality of your ceremony. Brides have walked down the aisle to the sounds of small orchestras playing the traditional wedding march as well as to the dulcet harmonies of kazoos. You may want your favorite local garage band to perform a special song or have your close friend with the good voice sing for you. Candles, ribbons, and flowers can all be used to add unique touches to your ceremony. And don't forget to consider what role the members of your wedding party, if any, will play. Certainly they may stand with you through the ceremony, but they can also be seated, read blessings, hold candles, or pass out flowers, depending on your needs.

Truly we are fortunate to live in a time when individual expression matters as much as, if not more than, tradition, giving you and your partner the freedom to create a ceremony that's truly meaningful because it reflects your creativity, beliefs, and personal style. While doing just what you want isn't easy—writing vows and researching traditions requires work—these personal touches can make your event all the more special.

Speedy Schmoozing

Having a receiving line either after the ceremony or before the reception, while hardly a requirement, is generally considered to be good etiquette. Sure it feels like an assembly line, but for many guests, it may be the one chance they get to congratulate you face-to-face. If it's a smaller wedding, the bride and groom can stand alone. For larger events, they can be flanked by their parents and wedding party. The best place for a receiving line is just outside the ceremony venue's exit (if it's an outdoor wedding, be creative) or along the entrance to the reception hall. Use this opportunity to make your guests feel welcome. Thank them for coming, and introduce them to parents or friends, as appropriate. Then relax and bask in all the warm wishes and glowing compliments that'll be coming your way.

chapter five

Fast Food

Menu planning? Describe your dream feast below.
Will it be sit-down, buffet, or other?

....

....

....

....

....

....

....

....

....

....

....

....

....

....

....

....

....

....

....

....

....

....

❀ Fast Food

Three months to go...
Hire the caterer.
Two months to go...
Choose a menu.
Reserve rentals and/or find alternatives.
One month to go...
Order dessert.
Buy the booze.
One week to go...
Confirm plans with venues, caterer, rental company, bakery.

The meal you serve at your wedding celebration is primarily dictated by the time of day. Early evening demands dinner of some variety, noontime is lunchtime, and the murky spaces in between can be filled with champagne and cake, cocktails and appetizers, or whatever your heart desires. Within those confines are many choices: buffet, sit-down, picnic, barbecue, potluck, bonfire, proper tea, pancake breakfast, and so on.

Style and Substance

Before you approach a caterer (loosely described here as the person who makes the food and drink happen), it's a good idea to have a sense of what style of reception you want. (If you're planning a hotel or package wedding where choosing the caterer isn't an option, it's still advisable to make your desires known.) The style of your reception should reflect your personalities and, because time is short, it should be fairly easy to pull off. If your heart is set on a dramatic re-creation of ancient Roman orgies or a reception chock-a-block with Martha Stewart–style minutiae, you may want to consider a longer engagement.

At the same time, a simple-yet-strong idea can go a long way. A picnic-style wedding can be easily expanded into a good-old-fashioned lawn party complete with parasols, croquet, and badminton. Your favorite Chinese restaurant can be lit up by bright paper lanterns, with lovely paper fans, personalized fortune cookies, and other fun trinkets distributed among guests. Snow cones spiked with vanilla-flavored vodka could be the signature beverage of a snow-white wedding at a friend's winter cabin.

Choosing a Caterer

When we think of caterers, we often just think of the food. But their work hardly stops there. They are responsible for your wait staff, and frequently other big stuff like linens, stemware, and even setting up the room. Hiring a caterer you like and trust is obviously very important, as is his or her willingness and ability to help you create your vision.

Caterers listed in popular publications and ones with mega-reputations are, like so many wedding vendors, booked far in advance. Freelance and small-event caterers are far more plentiful, thank goodness, and have greater flexibility than their big-time counterparts. As always, it helps to ask friends, family, and colleagues for recommendations. And never assume that the caterer you want is unavailable until you've picked up the phone and confirmed that for a fact. One small-event caterer says she and her staff would be able to put together a pretty decent wedding in a week or two as long as they had that day or evening free.

When interviewing caterers, the first question should always be whether they are available when you need them. After that, you'll want to ask for references, sample menus, and a free tasting (the yummy part!). If your location doesn't have an on-site kitchen, find out if they can prep everything off site or grill the food outdoors. (Be sure to find out if your site requires permits for things like grills.) Don't forget to ask for pictures of other events

they've catered! If you're all about having a funky-fresh wedding and from the looks of their photo album they've only worked on strictly traditional affairs, or vice-versa, then keep looking.

Ask the caterer for a range of prices that he or she charges per person. Find out what your caterer will and won't do, and what's included in the per-person charge. This varies a lot from place to place. Some caterers are essentially wedding planners, coordinating everything from seating to rentals and decor, while others do food and food alone. In your case, with so little time to plan, the more your caterer does, the better. Full-service caterers will have all the knowledge and experience of a professional planner—they've worked with the same musicians, venues, rental companies, and officiants—without the hefty fees most wedding coordinators charge.

If time is short, ask to see the menu for any events a caterer is working the day before or after your reception. If you like the menu, it will probably be a fairly simple thing to have the caterer make twice as much food—some for your event and some for the other (not leftovers!). This plan may make a busy caterer more willing and able to take on your event.

Questions to Ask Potential Caterers

- What does the total include? Just food? Or rentals, wait staff, setup and breakdown, and day-of coordination, too?

- What do you charge per person? What sort of menu would you create to fit our budget?

- What's the deposit and when is it due?

- When is a head count due?

- Are there time limits? What's the penalty for going overtime?

- Are you catering any other events on the day or weekend of our event?

- Who purchases alcohol and other beverages?

- Who is responsible for cleanup?

• Are tables, chairs, linens, flatware, and glasses included in the price, or will we have to rent them separately?

• Will you give us names and phone numbers of your recent clients, plus at least one facility where you've catered?

• If there isn't an on-site kitchen will you be able to prepare the food elsewhere or on an outdoor grill?

• Will additional permits for things like heat lamps or alcohol need to be purchased?

• What is your cancellation policy?

When Good Food Goes Bad

Food poisoning is a fairly unpleasant subject to bring up while talking of blessed nuptials and happily ever after, but in your rush to feed your guests, please don't overlook the kitchen. An unkempt, poorly organized kitchen is a breeding ground for nasty illnesses, which are not something you want to take along with you on your honeymoon—to say nothing of your poor guests!

To avoid a gastrointestinal tragedy, be sure to do the following:

• Check out where your food will be made. Be sure it's clean, organized, and pleasant.

• Ask around! (Caterers aren't likely to include people they've sickened among their references.)

• Trust your gut. If a place seems like the sort of place to play host to salmonella, don't go there.

• If you're truly worried, call the health department. They keep records of code violations.

• If your wedding is outside, avoid serving food that easily goes bad—anything egg-, milk-, or meat-based—or make sure adequate refrigeration is on hand.

• Don't forget to consult your guests about food allergies and restrictive diets.

• Serve food with accompanying labels or table cards informing guests of any ingredients that are common allergens (e.g., dairy, peanuts, or wheat).

When Caterers Aren't an Option

While a caterer's experience in planning events and menus is a valuable asset, his or her availability may be limited depending on when you're hoping to wed and how far out you are planning. And most caterers are not cheap. Fortunately there are plenty of other options.

THE RESTAURANT 'ROUND THE CORNER While the lovely Indian restaurant where you and your intended wooed and cooed your way to holy matrimony may not *usually* do weddings, that doesn't mean they won't. Is there a bar or restaurant that means a lot to you? Call them up. Chances are they'd be flattered to host such a special affair. Similarly, a morning ceremony at the courthouse could be topped off with a massive pancake breakfast at a kitschy diner. Your favorite restaurant may also be willing to bring the food to your location. Like caterers, restaurants are likely to charge by the head and will require you to stick with a prearranged menu.

TAKE-OUT Your local fancy-pants take-out palace or upscale grocery store is able to produce tray upon tray of cold cuts, pasta salads, pretty hors d'oeuvres, and delicious roasts in no time flat. Toss the food onto some pretty platters and you've got yourself an instant fancy buffet. For those on a budget, many caterers can simply drop off food for a help-yourself event. Rent some tables, chairs, plates, linens, and so on, and hire a freelance waiter or two to serve and clean up (call a caterer or friendly restaurant for recommendations, or place a classified ad).

POTLUCK It's true that potlucks tend to evoke dreadful memories of Aunt Henrietta's misshapen deviled eggs and Uncle Bob's "mystery-meat casserole," but it needn't be so. A reception is about celebrating with friends and families, so why not complete the party with your best friend's amazing artichoke dip, your father-in-law's mouthwatering slow-cooked spare ribs, and your grandma's famous apple pie—all the food you've grown up enjoying and will grow old enjoying together. All you need to do is make food assignments, and rent or borrow dishes and flatware, tables and chairs, and glasses and linens.

Amanda Castleman and John Franklin are no strangers to bad timing. It was bad timing when they met as students in Rome—both had to break up with other people back home in order to be together. Just as they were finally settling into their romance back home in Seattle, John got accepted to graduate school in London. Amanda could join him, but only as his wife. They dithered for a few weeks but finally decided to take the plunge. That left less than two months to plan the wedding *and* move to England.

With scarce time and few financial resources, the couple decided on a simple wedding at Amanda's parents' beachfront home in rural Washington state. Amanda bought a 1930s ball-gown for $40 at a Seattle antique store. She used her graphic-design skills to make invitations. John, an accomplished accordion player, serenaded his bride as she walked, arm in arm with her father, down the stairs leading to the beach. A friend, ordained over the Internet, performed the ceremony.

But the best part was yet to come. "My Italian American family cooked lasagna and focaccia, then spent a few hundred dollars on Chianti and Montepulciano. We insisted on a tiramisù wedding cake, which had to be flown in from Philadelphia, but otherwise it was all very low-key," Amanda recalls. Hungry guests happily gobbled down the heaps of steaming homemade lasagna, bread, salad, and tiramisù, following it with a red wine chaser. The luncheon feast, held at her parents' home, was followed by a taco-bar dinner, as the celebration went on into the night.

"Unfortunately, we left Seattle the day after the wedding. So our reception turned into a goodbye party, all sniffles and nostalgia. But it was the perfect ceremony for us —no tension, no artifice, no big bills. I recall the whole shebang costing about $450," she says.

So that long-distance relatives wouldn't have to make last-minute travel arrangements, Amanda and John invited only local friends and family to the main event, then stopped on the East Coast for some casual celebrating with family there before heading to London.

"We never would have married so quickly without the green-card pressure," Amanda says. "John and I approached the wedding very pragmatically, so it was a surprise how powerful the ceremony was. Exchanging vows in front of so many beloved people really cements the union."

PICNIC Deli sandwiches, fresh fruit, pasta salad, a bottle of chilled chardonnay, and some cheese and crackers. Yum! Picnics are romantic, simple, and easy to do—a great way to make the most of the beautiful setting afforded us by the great outdoors. Rent baskets and blankets—or buy a bunch for cheap from your local thrift shop and give them away as gifts when the festivities are over.

Rentals

If your reception venue or caterer doesn't offer tables, chairs, plates, linens, silverware, cups, and other items in the package, you will need to rent these things. Gazebos, aisle runners, forklifts, fondue pots, and pretty much anything else you can think of can also be rented. The price for all this stuff, between one-quarter and one-third of the total cost of the reception, can come as a shocker to the couple who's unprepared, and you will want to take the cost of rentals into account when you're choosing a location. A restaurant may sound expensive until you factor in what you'd pay to rent all those fancy forks and cocktail glasses.

If you had a ton of time, shopping around for deals on rentals would be recommended. Since you don't, you may want to go with whatever business your caterer prefers to work with; there are far better things to worry about. The bad news is that, as with all things wedding, your first choices may have been spoken for long ago, so be willing to compromise or move on to Plan B.

There are many ways to approach Plan B, also known as "The Fine Art of Rental Avoidance." First, there is borrowing. Someone you know belongs to some organization or club and chances are they have a bunch of tables and chairs you can borrow. As for plates, silverware, linens, and stemware, if the reception is really tiny, use your own or borrow Grandma's antique china and silver. Another idea is to have guests bring their own table setting, perfect in the instance of a picnic or similarly low-key gathering.

Second, while some wedding purists will strongly disagree, if the reception is very casual and you're comfortable doing it, go disposable. There are high-quality plates, napkins, and even champagne flutes that can be purchased for very little and easily forgotten afterward.

Finally, for something unique, hit the thrift stores and buy a ton of cheap, mismatched place settings. A used plate can go for as little as a quarter while a rental will run you $1.50 or more. If you have time, you can paint or stamp something personal onto them (using nontoxic paint or ink) and let the guests take them home as souvenirs.

The Scoop on Booze

Booze is the elixir of good times, and chances are your guests are expecting to get a little bit tipsy before the night is through. Perhaps you and your groom are teetotalers, but some of your hard-living guests may take offense if you don't pour at least a little champagne for the toast, and nondrinkers may get miffed if there isn't sparkling cider for them to raise in your honor. The jury is out on whether it's officially considered rude to serve free wine and beer but ask guests to pay for their own hard drinks. With all this said, it's completely up to you whether you serve alcohol, what types of alcohol you serve (hard or soft), when, and for how long. However, do make sure you're allowed to drink at your location. Some public places may forbid open containers, even if the container happens to be a crystal flute filled with the finest bubbly. Other locations will require permits.

Keeping the alcohol budget down doesn't mean you have to be a party pooper. Consider just serving specialty cocktails (his and hers are fun) rather than having a full bar, or include an open-bar cocktail hour right after the wedding. Folks can keep drinking the hard stuff after the cocktail hour, but they'll have to pay for it. Booze can easily be made to stretch a little further without the appearance of skimping. Buy some cheap wine and make sangria, or try a heady rum punch. Mimosas are always a treat.

If you are ordering wine and champagne (that is, if your reception venue doesn't require that you serve their wines), it's best to do it soon. A wine shop may have a couple cases of your favorite wine, but that doesn't mean the five or six you'll need are immediately available.

Oftentimes, wine orders can take several weeks to fill. Because wine is seasonal and produced in limited quantities, the amazing bottle of cabernet franc you had over dinner with your parents six months ago may not be available today. Nonvintage wines (often noted as N.V.) are a nice route to go. They tend to be not only cheaper but also consistent, so the case you buy at one place will taste the same as the case you buy at another. Of course, there are no rules against mixing it up a little. Throw out some cabernet, some merlot, and some rosé and let your guests choose what to drink.

Try big liquor stores first, since they have a larger back-room stock. If you choose to go through a smaller wine shop, which has the advantage of offering many foreign and hard-to-find bottles, ask for a guaranteed arrival time. Or try hitting up wineries directly; they often give big discounts for large orders and they know exactly how much of what vintage they have. Hard alcohol, beer, and nonalcoholic beverages are much easier to come by, thank goodness.

Cake

For some it's a monumental tradition on par with the exchanging of rings. For others, it's just dessert. Your and your groom's feelings about the cake will direct how much you spend on this confection or whether you serve it at all.

If you have your heart set on a towering work of sugary art, call a place that specializes in such creations and go in for a cake tasting. As with caterers, you might be able to hitch on to another bride's cake,

enabling the bakers to create two cakes at once (although a place
that does nothing but bake cakes probably won't need a ton of advance
warning). If you're really in a rush, ask if they have an abandoned
wedding cake stashed in the freezer, ready for you to serve (make sure
you give it enough time to thaw out!). Smaller bakeries and even
supermarkets produce some really delicious treats, so don't turn up
your nose at them. You could easily drop by your local grocery, purchase
three sizes of white cake, have the baker add some pretty flowers or
other decorations, *et voilà!*

Wedding cakes can cost hundreds or even thousands of dollars,
and most bakeries charge by the slice or per person rather than a flat
fee. At the same time there are plenty of folks out there who simply
aren't all that fond of cake. Not surprisingly, many couples are opting
for alternatives. Buy a bunch of cupcakes and top them with flowers.

Or build a doughnut tower. Have a relative make your or your groom's favorite childhood dessert. You can serve flan, sorbet with cookies, or some other frosting-free confection.

Finally, it's amazing how many brides and grooms report forgetting to eat at their wedding. Here it is, probably the most expensive meal they've ever served, and they don't even get to taste it. It's sick and wrong. Even if you do get to eat, you may find yourself so distracted that you barely remember it. So talk with your caterer. Have them make you a little to-go case to take with you. Then you can savor your wedding treats just a little bit longer.

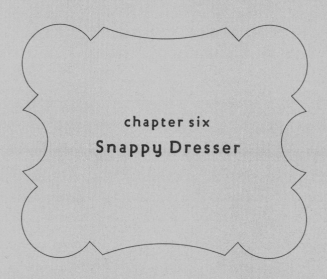

chapter six
Snappy Dresser

How do you measure up? Jot down your dress size; bust, hip, waist, and inseam measurements; and arm length here for easy reference.

....
....
....
....
....
....
....
....
....
....
....
....
....
....
....
....
....
....
....
....
....
....

❀ Snappy Dresser

Four months to go...
Shop for and buy or order wedding dress.
Choose and buy or order wedding rings.
Three months to go...
Select bridesmaids' dresses.
Two months to go...
Pick, buy, or rent groom's and groomsmen's outfits.
One month to go...
Schedule appointments for hair, makeup, nails, and other pampering.
One week to go...
Get rings sized, if necessary.
Have final dress fitting.
Do practice runs for hair and makeup.
One day to go...
Get manicure, pedicure, and other beauty treatments.

Brides have made their way down the aisle in all kinds of fabulous regalia. Fairy-tale princess dresses, jeans and cowgirl hats, wedding gowns carefully constructed out of glued-together doilies, birthday suits, Halloween costumes, and dramatic black velvet evening gowns. Grooms, too, have been known to have their fun, donning powder-blue tails or Elvis jumpsuits complete with gold fringe.

What you wear on your wedding day is an expression of your personality, your unique style, your desires, and how you wish to see yourself and be seen by others. If you choose a traditional white wedding gown, you probably see your marriage as part of a great legacy. If you choose to wear a sequined cocktail dress, then you're perhaps one who takes pride in flouting convention. Does white make you look washed out while red makes you look like a supermodel? Then understandably you may opt for a crimson wedding dress, because that's just what looks best.

When brides have the luxury of taking a year to plan, they can order their designer dress six months in advance, wait two months (or more) for it to arrive, and slog through several fittings before saying "I do." Their grooms can reserve tuxes months in advance or shop around in their spare time for the perfect suit. You two, of course, won't have the luxury of ordering the slow, old-fashioned way. Even if you have a couple of months to order a dress and wait around for it, do you have ample cushion in case something goes wrong, or do you have extra money to pay for a rush delivery? The more flexible you can be about the dress, his suit or tux, the bridesmaids' dresses, and groomsmen's outfits, the better. Fortunately, there are some excellent alternatives.

Shop Around the Clock!

While many of the following ideas apply to bridal gowns specifically, the advice holds for the groom's, bridesmaids', and groomsmen's attire, too.

OFF-THE-RACK While the majority of wedding dresses are tried on in a bridal boutique and then ordered, these same stores frequently have sales where they unload the dresses everyone's been trying on. The advantage of these warehouse, off-the-rack, or sample sales, as they're called, is that you can buy a traditional wedding gown and take it home the same day at a great price. Unfortunately, you may come across the perfect dress only to discover they don't have it in your size, it's damaged, or another bride has beaten you to it. Most off-the-rack dresses have suffered a smidgen of wear-and-tear in the dressing room.

Something Old, Something New . . .

If you're the traditional type, then you'll have something old, something new, something borrowed, and something blue with you on your wedding day. The custom, which originates with an old rhyme, is open to broad interpretation. To save time, you can double up. For example, grandma's antique earrings could count as something borrowed, old, and possibly blue. If the tradition isn't important to you, skip it, since worrying over such minor details will only cost you time.

BRIDESMAIDS' DRESSES FOR EVERYONE! Nearly all bridesmaids' dresses come in white. Many brides take this affordable, backdoor approach to getting a traditional gown. Be sure to leave time for it to be made, shipped, and custom fitted.

CUSTOM-MADE Getting a custom-made dress can be extremely costly and as slow as ordering one from a store, but not necessarily. If you want to save money, avoid people who bill themselves as wedding-gown designers and go for a seamstress who's talented, flexible, and experienced and charges an hourly fee that you can afford. When you meet with your dressmaker, come equipped with images, books, and anything else that demonstrates what you're hoping for. (Style is expressed in a wide variety of ways; sometimes a photograph of your fabulous living room or pictures from former parties will help you explain yourself to many people who'll be working on your wedding.) If you're going for a retro look, definitely check eBay and elsewhere online for antique dress patterns. You'll need to verify that your seamstress can do the work in a short period of time, get references, and peruse her portfolio. Make sure you get a written estimate and a contract before plunking down a deposit.

89

VINTAGE Going vintage has distinct advantages and disadvantages. There is an abundance of fabulous old dresses out there, and, unless you shop at Sotheby's, they don't come close to costing $5,000 or even $500. The downside of vintage is the challenge of finding the perfect dress in good condition that's also in your size or large enough to be taken in. You could visit every vintage store in a hundred-mile radius and find nothing, because fate has ordained that the dress of your dreams is located six hundred miles away in a city you never visit. The good news is that the Internet is home to a wealth of vintage stores as well as dresses for sale via auction sites like eBay. (See Point, Click, Buy Dress!, page 92).

CONSIGMENT/USED Former brides decide to sell their used wedding dresses for a variety of reasons. They may be divorced, or perhaps the wedding never happened. Most towns and cities have consignment shops that specialize in fancy garb. If you're not superstitious, buying used can mean getting a great deal on a super-fancy gown. If you're looking for something other than the traditional white satin-and-tulle confection, these shops can be a jackpot. Consignment shops are a great resource not only for wedding dresses and evening gowns but also for bridesmaids' dresses, men's suits, tuxedos, accessories, and more.

RENTALS For years, grooms have happily rented their tuxes and returned them the next day. So why do so many brides snub the idea of doing the same? For people who think spending a small fortune on an outfit they may wear only once is simply foolish, renting is a great alternative. Wedding gowns and dresses of all kinds can be borrowed for a small sum from places that specialize in such arrangements. Many theater companies and costume shops, too, own a wealth of gorgeous and unique garments that can be borrowed at a price. Men renting tuxes will want to reserve as far in advance as possible. Again, avoiding rush periods, such as around high-school proms or weekends in June, will make it easier to get exactly what you want.

MOM'S CLOSET There is a long and rich tradition of brides borrowing the wedding dresses worn by their mothers or grandmothers. If you have looked lovingly upon old family wedding pictures and would like to add memories of your own to the ancestral history, it would certainly not hurt to ask. Likely, your mom or grandma or even aunt will gladly surrender her dress and maybe even let you customize it as needed. Similarly, you may have a good friend who is willing to lend her wedding dress for your big day.

YOUR CLOSET Do you own a fabulous dress that you rarely have occasion to wear, that your fiancé would die to see you wear, and that, frankly, you can't get enough of as well? Perhaps you own a dress of particular sentimental value that can be repurposed for a very personal wedding outfit. Does your groom have a dashing suit that he rarely gets to wear? There's no hard-and-fast rule that says you have to go out and buy something specifically for your wedding, especially when there's something perfect right under your nose. Bridesmaids and groomsmen, especially, will be grateful if they can just select something that they already own.

PROM DRESSES, BALL GOWNS, AND OTHER FANCY STUFF

The dress of your dreams may be no farther away than your friendly local mall. A great prom dress or a gorgeous gown selected from the special-occasions section of your local department store can often easily pass for a wedding gown or bridesmaid's dress, at a fraction of the cost. Or, if you want a pulled-together look but don't necessarily want everyone to wear the same shade of satin, vintage suits, the preferred garb of '50s brides, are an easy-to-find and stylish alternative to a wedding dress or bridesmaids' outfits. In short, looking for great outfits in places other than bridal boutiques can yield great results for less money, time, and hassle.

Rings!

Many of the rules that apply to buying a wedding dress also apply to purchasing rings. Rings that are ordered may take two months or longer to arrive. If you are hoping to have your rings custom-made, you must

The Internet has opened up an inordinate number of shopping opportunities for engaged couples. There are hundreds of boutiques and vintage stores, which you'd never be able to visit in person, now open twenty-four hours a day anywhere there's a phone line and a modem. Buying bridal dresses and related accessories has become so popular on eBay that the popular auction site devotes an entire shopping area to weddings.

While most people online are good, honest folks, there are a few nut jobs out there, so buyer beware, especially on auction sites. At the same time, careful purchasing can mean scoring a great pair of shoes, a fabulous dress, an elegant tiara, or the perfect veil. It can be well worth the risk.

The "I Do's" of Online Shopping

- Do go with what you know. If you've always looked fabulous in a boat neckline, then you know a dress with this cut will suit you. The Internet is not the place to experiment with a new look.

- Do have a strong sense of what you're looking for. If there's a special name for the cut of dress you desire or the type of sleeves you want, make sure to include it in searches.

- Do know your measurements ahead of time. Start with bust, waist, and hips, but also get your inseam, arm length, and other measurements. Consult size charts *before* buying.

- When buying from an auction site, do check out the seller's rating to be sure other customers have been satisfied with their purchases.

- Do buy something a little larger than the size you need. It's easier to take something in than to let it out.

- Do inspect the pictures of the merchandise thoroughly before buying and ask questions of the seller.

- Do ask for a guaranteed arrival date for your gown and other items. Nothing's more stressful than wondering whether they will arrive on time.

Some good places to start your online shopping adventure are listed in the Resources section of this book.

allow at least two months to research styles, find the right designer, and review several iterations of the design before you get exactly what you want. The same guidelines for hiring a seamstress to design and make your dress apply here (see page 89). You can take a used or vintage ring home with you the day you buy it (unless you get it at an auction Web site), but you may need to look around for a long time before finding the perfect one for you.

At the same time, rings are in plentiful supply. Simple gold bands can be bought for as little as $40. When shopping for new rings, ask the jeweler which ones are available right away and which need to be ordered. Re-sizing a ring that's not too ornate can usually be done in a day. The same fast turnaround time goes for engraving.

If you are really short on time or money, consider wearing temporary wedding rings until you can get the ones you really want. After all, it's the wearing of the ring, rather than the object itself, that really matters.

Quick Makeover

Makeup, hair, nails, facials. Some ladies just love to primp, while others are happy with a good scrub now and then. While getting the full-blown movie-star treatment certainly isn't the reason a girl gets married, pampering can certainly make a gal feel a little more confident, relaxed, and drop-dead gorgeous. If you know your hairdresser gets booked up a month in advance, be sure to call him or her as soon as you have a date picked. If you're a good customer, he or she may be willing to rearrange his or her schedule to create your special-day 'do.

To get the most out of your last-minute pampering, take the following advice:

• Now is not the best time to experiment with your look or try new products. Go with what you know looks good on you, and try out new hair colors and facial masks when you have the luxury of recovery time.

• Schedule a practice hair and makeup session with your beautician a few days to a few weeks before the wedding.

• Be sure to wax no later than a couple of days before your event, to make sure any redness or breakouts have time to go away.

• Haircuts and dye jobs often look best if given a week or two to grow out or mellow. Manicures and pedicures, on the other hand, look great the day of.

• A Brazilian wax (that's the bikini line plus a bit —OK, a lot—off the sides) is rumored to spice up the honeymoon, even if you've only been sleeping together for the past twelve years.

• You're stressed. It's understandable. But take care of yourself! Lots of rest, a healthy diet, and exercise will do for your complexion what no spa can.

It's been said that no bride looks bad on her wedding day. The joy and excitement, the adrenaline, and the primping all go a long way toward creating a natural glow that will be far more memorable than any dress, pedicure, or bouquet. In other words, you could roll out of bed on your wedding day and show up an hour later in a well-worn sundress, or you could spend a month getting your teeth bleached and face injected with Botox, and the result would be pretty much the same.

After Jennifer Lynch, a chef, and Daniel Haskovec, a software programmer, decided to get married, they didn't see much need to prolong the engagement. "It was June and he wanted to get married in June," Jennifer recalls. That was a bit impractical, so they decided on early October instead, which came after the Burning Man art festival that the couple attend yearly.

They picked a place where they'd already attended a wedding and several house-music dance parties. "We'd been to the space a lot of times and we knew it was pretty perfect and inexpensive to rent," Jennifer says. She knew there would also be little interference from the managers of the location, for example, requirements that a specific caterer be used. Friends were tapped to help out with every aspect of the party. A cook friend did the catering, another made the cake, and yet another designed the invitations. Jennifer and a pal picked up flowers at the flower market the day before and her friend created the floral arrangements.

Jennifer's dress also came courtesy of a friend who happened to be an amazing seamstress. The two got together a month before the wedding and pored over magazines and books, picking out what they liked and didn't like. Then they shopped for fabric and the seamstress went to work. What they came up with was stunning—a dramatic, tongue-in-cheek play on the traditional wedding dress.

The first layer was a simple green silk underdress with spaghetti straps that Jennifer wore to the cocktail party that preceded the ceremony. After that, a corset of silvery seatbelt straps, melted together and tied with ribbon through grommets, was added. A sheer silver A-line skirt was attached with further ribbons and grommets. French wire was woven in to create a bustle.

"I felt like an alien queen," Jennifer recalls. So dramatic was her dress, in fact, that she had Dan dye his hair red so she wouldn't be the only one standing out at the altar.

Of course, designing and creating a dress in a month isn't exactly easy. Jennifer was still having adjustments made as late as one o'clock in the morning two days before the wedding. On the day of, the seamstress accidentally cut an eight-inch gash in the hem while adding some finishing touches. "I didn't notice. She just basted it up and told me at the end of the wedding," Jennifer says.

All in all, everything went beautifully, something Jennifer says is a real tribute to her friends. "In the absence of organized religion, your friends are what's true. That's how we wrote our ceremony. We made it clear that the people who came to our wedding were our actual family and the closest thing to God that we know of."

chapter seven
Instant Messaging

Word up! Use the space here to write a rough draft
of what your invitation will say.

....
....
....
....
....
....
....
....
....
....
....
....
....
....
....
....
....
....
....
....
....
....

🌸 Instant Messaging

Three months to go...
Order invitations and personalized items.
Two months to go...
Order and send "save the date" cards.
Order thank-you notes.
Register for gifts.
Build a wedding Web site.
One month to go...
Address and mail invitations.

Presumably, you've informed key people of the essentials well before starting work on the invitations. Now the time for more formal communication has come—be it printed on embossed vellum wrapped with tissue and delivered via singing telegram, or hastily conveyed over the phone. Invitations are a vehicle for communicating a lot of information to your guests. They also can set a tone. An email invite hints at a decidedly casual wedding, while professional printing implies something a bit more chichi. Eco-friendly couples may act on their views by printing on recycled paper. Many fancy invites double as mementos.

Save the Date and Save Your Butt!

The save-the-date card is a recently evolved tradition that makes a lot of sense, especially if your wedding guest list is fairly long or geographically diverse. If you have two months or more before the big day, sending out a cheap and easy postcard to friends and relatives will ensure that they know when you're getting married, so they can start making plans well before the official invite arrives. You, meanwhile, have bought yourself some breathing room to prepare your invitations. If something delays the invitations, no sweat! You've already given people enough warning.

Browse through your local office-supply store. In recent years, numerous software programs and paper materials have emerged that make it easy to design your own cards. Most word-processing software today has a feature allowing you to create cards, which can then be printed out on a desktop printer or taken to a copy shop to be placed on high-quality stock (that's fancy printers' talk for nice paper). Online there are a plentitude of print shops that let you upload (that's geek talk for placing an image and text online; any Web site worth its salt will walk you through this process) artwork and text; they print the postcards and you can send them right away. For weddings that are being planned just a week or less in advance, or when informing people of an elopement, a phone call is best—you won't have time to do more. If you place yourself in the low-tech category, there's nothing wrong with handaddressing a few pretty postcards from your local museum gift shop or stationery store, adding the crucial note saying, "We're getting married," when, and where.

There is much debate today over whether it's rude, crude, or socially unacceptable to use email or a Web site for invitations and other official wedding communication. Truly there is something to be said for the special feeling one gets when a pretty envelope arrives in the mail. Paper and a stamp are unquestionably more intimate than the computer's announcement, "You've got mail!" Then again, an interactive bells-and-whistles Web invite complete with Java script and Flash animation might best represent your personalities and professions. A save-the-date email followed by an official paper-and-ink invite may ruffle a few crusty old feathers, but not many. You'll still have to go the old-fashioned route for those folks who haven't jumped on the online bandwagon. As always, do whatever feels right and works best.

Note to the freaked-out reader: Admittedly this chapter is fairly technology intensive. Those of you reading this who are computerless or technophobic may already be adding the price of a laptop and software lessons into the wedding budget, or perhaps you are simply despairing. Fear not! Only in the last decade have email and Web sites been introduced into the parade of wedding paraphernalia. While there's no denying that technology can help speed things up in a lot of ways, certainly many brides and grooms before you have gotten by without pointing and clicking, and so can you.

Couples who've been together for a while or who simply want to forgo the formalities of an official wedding may want to consider having a surprise wedding.

The set up: Tell family and friends that you are throwing a very special party (an anniversary or holiday is a good excuse) that it's important for them to attend. One decadent couple wrapped invites in silk scarves to indicate that it wasn't going to be an ordinary celebration.

Preparations: Hire a caterer, photographer, officiant, and entertainment as you would for any special party.

Surprise! Once your guests have settled in, say you have an announcement, and let the surprise ceremony begin.

Building a Wedding Web Site

The wedding Web site is fast becoming a standard part of many nuptials. For an instant wedding it can be of invaluable help. Rather than having to make maps for all your guests, you can direct guests to click on your site and print one for themselves. Important information on accommodations that often clutters invitation envelopes can be communicated en masse via the Internet. It's a lovely way to express yourselves, too, with pictures from your lives or the story of how you two crazy kids first met.

There was a time when building a Web site required coding skills, but no more. Hooray! For those with fewer technical skills than your eighty-year-old great-grandma, several Web sites allow you to just fill in the information, pick from a menu of styles, and press send. They do all the work from there. If you are more technically skilled, try one of the many software programs that allow you to design a Web site without knowing the slightest bit of code. If you make your own, definitely enlist a geeky friend to help you get the information off your computer and onto the Internet.

- With some basic software, some free server space (this often comes with your home email address), and the help of a tech-savvy pal, putting up a Web site from scratch can be fun and easy.

- Decide what it'll say. Spend some time with your honey brainstorming what to include on your Web site. Will it just be practical information or something fun? Do you want to include pictures?

- Get the needed software. Before you spend money, check your hard drive. New computers often come with Web-design software. Windows Office Suite now comes with Front Page, an easy-to-use Web-site-building program. If you find yourself lacking for these, head to your friendly neighborhood electronics store and ask for their con-sumer-level Web design program. (See Resources at the end of the book for recommendations.)

- Find a host. If you have an email account at home, free Web space may be part of the package. Call your Internet Service Provider to find out whether this is the case. Otherwise, search online for a basic hosting package (often as low as $10 a month; see Resources) or ask a Web-savvy friend if you can throw your files onto his or her Web site for a little while.

- Spread the word! What good is a Web site if nobody knows how to find it? Send an email letting people know you have a Web site and what they can find there. Alert them whenever the site is updated.

What should this wedding Web site include? While your classy invite may give the whens and wheres of your event, the Web site serves to fill in the blanks. Provide directions and a map. Add a link from your Web site to online gift registries, which are now standard at most large retail concerns. (Although it is still considered rude in some circles for the bride or groom to so much as whisper to people where they are registered, other couples consider it polite to let people know.) If guests are traveling a long way, it might be nice to recommend restaurants and sight-seeing excursions for them to enjoy during their visit. Where to find low airfares, the story of how you met, and other kinds of content are just icing on the cake. After the wedding is over, you can use your Web site to share photographs from the event.

Invites on the Double!

If you go to the usual wedding-invitation vendors—as with your local stationery store or anyone advertising in popular bridal magazines—the time between when you order your wedding invitations and when they arrive will be at least a month and possibly as long as two months, and Lord help you if any mistakes are made. Rush orders can cost you dearly, often as much as 50 percent on top of the going rate. Even online sites, often simply Web extensions of old-fashioned invitation companies, hew to this glacial schedule.

The good news is an invitation, like so many things wedding, no longer has to be traditional and formal. Instead of being a black-and-white, calligraphy-laden, engraved document, it can reflect your personalities in a number of ways, and this freedom also means that you no longer have to depend on traditional wedding stationery vendors. A design-savvy friend can create a wedding logo for you, perhaps a cute caricature of you two or a stylized rendering of your initials, to emblazon on your stationery. Clip art is plentiful and cheap and can be a good source of images that match your wedding theme or style. One San Francisco couple had their invites designed after they'd picked a spot but before they'd chosen a date, so they used a rubber date stamp (think library) to add that information later.

Of course, there are a handful of businesses that do cater to last-minute brides, providing quick printing without heavy fees. (See Resources section.) Another option is to hire a printer that does a lot of work for businesses—as in business cards, stationery, and even key chains. Companies, unlike brides, are in a position to demand faster turnaround times, so using a printer that caters to the biz world will make it more likely that you'll get your invites on time. An added benefit of using a business printer is that you can have them do your favors, too. Instead of paying wedding prices and enduring industry wait times to have your date engraved on a chocolate bar, peruse their selection of pens, key chains, candles, screensavers, hats, and so on—all of which can be personalized for a nominal fee.

While wedding-invite companies now offer an increasing range of designs, graphics, and options, if you're looking for something truly special, you will have to do it yourself or hire a graphic designer. Creating an invite from scratch will demand more of your time to begin with, but you'll end up with a highly personal missive that says just what you want to say. Again, there are a number of programs and packages now sold in office-supply stores that enable you to create and print perfectly acceptable invites. Many photocopy stores have benefited from improved copier technology in recent years, so another option may be to go to one of these storefronts with a disk and some specifications in hand and let them do it. The one downside of photocopiers as well as most desktop printers is that the ink isn't permanent, leaving you with a faded souvenir from your wedding years down the line.

Thank-you notes that match your wedding invitations are certainly nice. If you go this route, you'll want to have them printed with all your other stationery, because small orders tend to cost more than big orders.

For uniqueness and style, Summer Lopez and Kim Abrams's wedding invitations definitely took the prize. Since many of the people they were inviting to their wedding didn't know the story of how they met and got engaged, the couple decided their invites should function as a story line chronicling milestones in their relationship. They provided an artistic friend with a simple storyboard and some photographs. She created a multipage comic-book-style invitation, which they then printed at a local copy shop onto fancy paper and painstakingly assembled—each page of the story in order—by hand.

"With everything done, we walked to the corner mailbox, happily dropped in our lovingly crafted invitations, and skipped off hand in hand, completely unaware that the stickers holding together the envelopes were as weak as our dog's sense of modesty and that the invitations were exploding open and dumping their contents all over the mailbox at that very moment," recalls Kim, who despite his feminine name is very much a man.

Even worse, the postal workers tried to salvage the situation by stuffing random pieces of the invites into envelopes, so some people got duplicate invitations, while others got empty envelopes, and others received nothing at all. The only thing Kim and Summer could do was start the whole process over—printing, assembling, and mailing, this time with some serious sticky holding it together. With little time to spare at this point, they asked people to R.S.V.P. via email or phone.

Of course, matching isn't necessary. You can simply buy a bunch of thank-you cards from your local stationery store and use those. Or print your own. Emailed thank-you notes are definitely a no-no. If people go to the trouble of buying you a gift, the least you can do is thank them with a handwritten note. What kind of note is entirely up to you. It's the contents that count.

Speaking of handwriting, few wedding tasks are more time-consuming and flat-out boring as addressing all those envelopes by hand. Like many things, invitation etiquette is relaxing. Many couples find it perfectly acceptable to print or hand-address invitations at home. But if your budget allows for it, hiring a professional calligrapher to do the dirty work can be a huge time-saver. You can expect to spend between $2.50 and $5.00 per envelope for very basic calligraphy. An experienced calligrapher usually finishes the job in ten to fourteen days, but can do rush jobs for an extra fee. The stationery store where you buy your invitations can often recommend calligraphers, or check your local listings. As always, be sure to ask for references and get a contract in writing.

There's nothing like a printed invite to kick in the fact that this wedding is for real. Once those puppies are printed, addressed, and stamped, turning back is going to be very difficult. For this reason, the paper aspect of a wedding can be very emotional and exciting. Opening a mailbox full of dainty response cards is truly thrilling. So while putting together and printing the invitations may be difficult, in the end it's totally worth it.

Booty!

While dithering over china patterns and comparing coffeemakers may sound like a waste of time when there are so many other things to do before your wedding, registering for gifts is a good thing. First, it saves time later, since you don't want to spend your first months together at the returns window of your local department store.

Second, protocol dictates that guests have an entire year to send a gift to a couple (although the couple should respond with a thank-you note within one month of receiving each gift). So even if there's scarce time *before* the wedding for people to shop for gifts, the registry can still be used long after you've said "I do."

Last, registering for gifts is easier than ever these days. If you have Web access, you don't even have to leave your home. Plenty of stores let you pick your gifts online, allow guests to shop for them in-store or on the Web, and ship them to you directly. If you do need to go to a brick-and-mortar store, registering shouldn't take more than an afternoon. When the booty starts rolling in, you'll be glad you took the time.

chapter eight
Lights, Camera, Action!

Don't forget to say cheese! Write down all the pictures you'll
want taken and the songs you'll want playin'.

....
....
....
....
....
....
....
....
....
....
....
....
....
....
....
....
....
....
....
....
....
....
....
....

🏵 Lights, Camera, Action!

Three months to go...
~~
Book a photographer.
Two months to go...
~~
Book musicians and other entertainment.
Hire a florist and plan flowers.
One week to go...
~~
Visit site with photographer and discuss picture list.
Confirm plans with florist and entertainers.

A wedding reception is, after all, just a big party, and if you want to make a splash, you'll need all the amenities—fabulous entertainment, festive decor, and a gadfly photographer to document every happy moment. Although these three components—entertainment, decorations, and pictures—are quite different from one another, the tactics for obtaining them in a hurry are remarkably similar.

Not that you *need* any of these things, by the way. You could just as easily head to city hall, then go out to dinner at a favorite restaurant with a friend taking snapshots and your father's giddy toasts providing the laughter. In this case, feel free to skip ahead to the next chapter. After all, you're short on time!

But if you are in the market for any of these services, always call your first choices on the off chance they're available to work on the day of your event. Creative professionals are often willing to take on an extra gig, for they do not always know when the next one will come along. If your event takes place on an off-night, it's all the more likely they'll be free. If your first choice isn't available, get recommendations. Professional organizations, both wedding-related and skill-related, often have listings for local talents who've had to jump through a few rigorous hoops to be included. If you're clueless about where to start looking, these groups can be a great resource. And don't hesitate to look outside of your town (within reason). All the local talent may be booked, but someone just as good who's living in the suburbs fifty miles away could be available.

Good musicians, photographers, and florists are often to be found in places other than the yellow pages. Schools and businesses are treasure troves of talented people. If you're lucky, a photography professor or local photojournalist may be willing to freelance. A class of advanced horticulture students might provide you with just as lovely a bouquet as your local florist at a fraction of the cost. The nearby college could be home to a genius violinist who's paying for her schooling by performing at weddings and other events. Even street musicians, if they're good, can be employed to play a gig. If you're in a city with a large Hispanic population, for example, you can often find mariachis standing on street corners in hopes of landing a last-minute job.

As always, it's good to tap your friends—

but be careful. There are too many stories floating around about couples who hired a friend to take their wedding photos or bake the cake, only to end up with a stack of blurry pictures or a shapeless mound of mealy confection and, even worse, a strained friendship. Of course, if you have a friend who happens to work as a wedding photographer or floral designer or musician and this person's already planning to be at your wedding, he or she probably won't say no to taking on the job (maybe even as a gift or at a discount). A pal with a green thumb will most likely be flattered if you ask her to arrange roses from her garden for your special day. Of course, a close buddy might prefer to quaff champagne and mingle instead of working at your event. And, if things do go terribly awry, it could hurt the friendship. Sometimes it's better to preserve the relationship and let a pro handle the work, so use your best judgment.

Nobody thinks twice about hiring a photographer or a videographer to cover an *entire* event, so why do so few people consider moving flowers from chapel to banquet hall or having the musicians play at both locations? Hiring one set of entertainers and ordering one set of flowers saves you money while reducing the amount of time you have to spend looking for talent and choosing designs. Move floral arrangements from

Stephan Cox and Lori Culwell are not much for pomp and circumstance. Their courtship began on a crowded train after Stephan practically stepped on Lori's lunch. He first brought up the *M* word in a strip club, where (they swear!) they were just entertaining a cousin. And when it came to getting married, they were all set to stop off at city hall when their parents intervened and asked that they at least have a small wedding for family and friends.

"We listened to everyone else and got all stressed out. Suddenly I was like, 'Do I have to buy a brides' magazine?' I considered myself too ironic for that," Lori recalls.

She did eventually buy a bridal magazine and what she read shocked her—namely, the price tag. From then on out, she says, "It became a game. We tried to find cool things we could do that wouldn't be so ridiculously expensive."

Although the two were officially engaged in February, they didn't decide on a location until six weeks before the event took place in September. Through Lori's dad, they found an officers' yacht club with a beautiful view that they could have all day for $125. The dress came from Nordstrom Rack. Kazoos were handed out to wedding guests for a giggle-inducing rendition of "Here Comes the Bride," and a friend acted as DJ. A local deli dropped off the food, which was served buffet style. Invitations were ordered over the phone and rushed out. An amateur photographer who was working on her portfolio took pictures for $150. Lori's best friend and maid of honor picked up flowers from the local flower market and made simple but lovely arrangements. All told, the wedding came to around $2,000.

"I don't mean to make it sound easy, because it wasn't, but everything was flowing. What made that happen is we didn't have all those really rigid standards," says Lori. "We ordered a cake and it was done in a week. We just needed a really big cake. Who cares what it looks like?"

In the end, Lori says, the wedding had everything the magazine said it should have, but what makes the couple happy is that they ignored everyone's advice and did things their way.

113

the ceremony to the reception. Have the singer perform before the ceremony, during, and after. Once you find people who are good, milk 'em for all they've got!

If you are on a very tight budget, or if you simply want to do it up differently, you may need to explore viable alternatives to the traditional wedding vendors. Florists, photographers, and musicians are great, but they rarely come cheap. Different options will be explored as we delve into each of these areas a little more deeply.

Snap Shots

Long after the last glass of bubbly has been consumed, the confetti swept away, and the final thank-you note slipped into the mailbox, there will be pictures. (There may also be a video, if you are so inclined; all the same advice applies.) Your photographs will be one of the few aspects of your event that are lasting. For this reason, most wedding coordinators say that this is one area where a couple should never cut corners. At the same time, top wedding photographers are booked months and even years in advance and don't bat an eyelid at charging $15,000 for their services. So, obviously, you may have no choice but to go around the system.

Wedding photography, though often looked down upon within photographic circles, is a difficult craft to master. A wedding photographer must be gifted at both portraiture and candid shots. He must work under all sorts of lighting conditions and be in multiple places at once. She is friendly, affable, and can elicit genuine smiles from the sternest of relatives. A good photographer knows how to make short people look tall and fat folks appear skinny, and how to keep shadows off of Uncle Gordon's shapely face. All this is done while lugging heavy equipment; switching film, cameras, and lenses; and taking hundreds of perfect pictures. No wedding photographer gets good at this overnight. It takes practice, lots of it. And it takes equipment—several professional-level cameras, batteries, film, a darkroom, flashbulbs, studio backdrops, and more.

In short, few students or even photographic assistants are going to have what you need. Then again, maybe you're not looking for glossy stills of your entire family standing rigidly in a row, or glamour shots of your spiffy rings. Find a compromise that works for you. For example, you could have a few formal shots taken ahead of time at a portrait photographer's studio or on site and hand over the wedding-day shooting to a talented friend. Or try some of the options discussed at the beginning of this chapter—hiring a professor, photojournalist, or photo assistant. And don't worry if your photographer doesn't get every shot you are hoping for. Chances are that a shutterbug friend or relative will be able to fill in the gaps.

When interviewing photographers, there are a number of additional things you'll want to ask them about. Do they shoot in black-and-white, color, or both? Do they have a specialty? Some photographers excel at taking formal portraits, while others are adept at capturing the day with candid shots. It's important to find out whether the photographer keeps the negatives or whether they belong to you. Is a substitute on call if your photographer has a personal emergency and is unable to work on the day of the wedding? Inspect the contract carefully. What is included in your package? Prints? A nicely arranged album? What will you be charged extra for and how much?

Here's a word on those disposable cameras, which now seem to be an obligatory component of every wedding. While in theory it's nice to have guests take pictures—after all, there are more of them and, hence, they will capture more moments than just one photographer can—more often than not, these cameras yield poor-quality pictures, especially when taken by amateurs. Worse, the disposables fall into the hands of children and you end up paying for six dozen blurry shots of people's feet. Given the initial expense of these cameras and the cost of developing the film, you may want to just let the folks who enjoy taking pictures bring their own cameras and ask them for duplicates.

Breezy Decorating

Ordering flowers is wonderfully uncomplicated and can easily be done last minute. In fact, if you're not ordering a ton of flowers, there's no need to do anything in advance. Have someone pick up what you need and make arrangements last minute. Brides have stopped off at flower shops, grocery stores, and farmers' markets as late as the morning of the event to gather materials for tabletop arrangements and bouquets. Some florists need as little as two days' advance notice to take an order and do your arrangements—as long as you're not asking for a huge amount of work or flowers that aren't currently in season. Friends' gardens can also be a wonderful resource for the penny-pincher. Make the most of cheap flowers by clipping their petals and spreading them around tables or in place of an aisle runner. Floral arrangements can be as expensive and extensive or as cheap and minimal as you want and still look amazing, so do what you wish.

Blossoms are easily shared, too. Churches usually have fresh flowers brought in weekly; see if they can be brought early for your event. If there's another wedding in your venue that day, it can't hurt to call and discuss whether sharing is an option; certainly some brides will bristle at the suggestion, but others will appreciate the opportunity to reduce costs.

The farther away from traditional arrangements you veer, the easier and more interesting your decor can get. Vases, for example, don't *have*

Hooray for Bouquets!

Traditionally, close family members and the wedding party are gussied up with flowers to set them apart from the other guests. Here's a breakdown of who gets which flowers.

• Bride and bridesmaids: bouquets (plus, possibly, a "tossing bouquet")

• Groom, groomsmen, ushers, fathers, and grandfathers: boutonnieres

• Mothers, grandmothers, and junior bridesmaids: corsages

to be bought. Empty wine bottles, antique urns, mason jars, wicker baskets, and goldfish bowls all do fabulously in a pinch. And who says you need flowers at all? Fill the goldfish bowl with goldfish, the mason jars with live fireflies. Rent pretty potted plants from a local nursery, or instead arrange the food in a centerpiece-worthy display. Candles are an illuminating and mood-setting alternative or addition to flowers. Simple white holiday lights can add a lot of beauty to a room. In a postcard setting with a dramatic view, sometimes it's better to let the environment supply the eye candy. Why upstage nature? Another oft-made suggestion is to simply use a location's preexisting decor, which is especially easy during the holidays when hotels and restaurants go all out.

Entertainment

When people consider their wedding entertainment, they tend to limit themselves to the choice between band and DJ. As with so many things, these acts might be difficult to book at the last minute. Fortunately there's an abundance of other options. So in addition to the entertainment suggestions at the beginning of this chapter—hiring mariachis, con-tracting with student musicians or instructors, and asking a friend to play music or spin records—here are some alternatives you may want to consider:

- Call up favorite cafes and bars and ask for band and DJ recommendations.

- Burn CDs of your favorite music. (See Be Your Own DJ below.)

- If there's a cultural heritage you and your groom want to highlight, call up the local cultural center and see if there's a dance troupe or other act that can provide dinner entertainment.

- Hire a professional storyteller to regale guests with tales of medieval romance, Renaissance Faire–style. Or have a stand-up comic do a routine on love and marriage.

- Use actors or acting students wearing period costumes to bring to life the theme of your reception—such as a Roman feast or Victorian tea party.

- If you have adorable children or nephews and nieces, ask them to put on a play telling the story of your romance.

Be Your Own DJ

Many computers now come equipped with a built-in CD burner, making it much easier to make custom mixes of your favorite music. If you don't have such a computer, ask around to see if someone you know does. Custom CDs can also now be ordered online or via phone.

Make a song list with your fiancé, including personal anthems and shared favorites. Gather together all the CDs that have the songs you want on them, and borrow from friends those that you don't already own. Think about how you want them arranged. One slow song for every three fast songs? Don't forget to include the first dance, if you're having one! Then familiarize yourself with the needed software. There are a lot of different kinds out there and they're all a little different, so don't assume you know what you're doing. As with all things tech, ask a computer-savvy friend or coworker for help if you need it. Make enough CDs to cover the period of time you'll want music playing.

The best part about making a CD is that the CDs themselves are really cheap, so once you've arranged everything, you can burn extra copies to give away as favors.

- Karaoke machine! Let your friends and family serenade you with their goofy renditions of love songs.

- Consider having a slide show, documenting your childhoods, culminating in your courtship and marriage. For hard-core geeks, a PowerPoint presentation projected onto the wall could provide a hilarious spectacle.

Down with Perfect!

When you're investing so much time and energy in one event, when all your family and friends are gathering expectantly for your big day, it is tempting to want everything to be *perfect.* Perfect pictures. Perfect flowers. Perfect dress. Perfect weather. In the midst of the prewedding frazzle, it can be easy to overlook the fact that the *inevitable* little mishap that's got you all bent out of shape will become a hilarious anecdote to be enjoyed over many years of retelling.

So if, on your wedding day or beforehand, you find yourself short of breath because the musician isn't returning your phone calls, your grandpa is complaining about where he's standing during the photo shoot, you can't find your grandma's crystal champagne flutes, your dream flowers for your bouquet are out of stock, or your dress needs to be let out thanks to that second piece of bridal-shower cake, take a deep breath and remember that there's no such thing as perfect. No wedding is perfect, just as there are no perfect people, no perfect marriages, no perfect days. What you've got is you and your husband-to-be and real life, which you're both lucky enough to be figuring out together.

Focus on that and go with the flow. You'll have much more fun.

chapter nine
Fast Getaways

Going someplace? Stash the names and numbers of travel agents, hotels, airlines, and other helpful info here.

❀ Fast Getaways

One month to go...
Arrange to take time off work.
Update passport/visa, if necessary.
Book wedding-day and honeymoon transportation and lodging.
One week to go...
Confirm travel plans.

The wedding has come to an end. The caterer has been paid; the decorations have been cleared away. You've kissed your grandma good-bye at least six times, you've sent your bridesmaids off with their gifts, and you and your husband haven't had a moment alone in the last two hours. For the past several weeks you've done nothing but plan, plan, plan, and now, all too quickly, it's over. Your brain is a jumble of disjointed memories. And speaking of joints, yours are aching from all that boogying. You're completely, thoroughly, and totally pooped. Now there is but one thing left to do: honeymoon.

The honeymoon can be both a blessing and a curse. In the midst of planning a wedding so last-minute-like, it may seem like a big pain to add "call travel agent" to your already too long "To Do" list. After expending enormous amounts of energy on organizing and celebrating—to say nothing of the emotional weight of the commitment itself—the last thing you may want to do is pack a suitcase and get on a plane. But it's for these very reasons that you ought to get away, even if it's just for a few nights at the retro Motor Inn down the road. Not only do you *need* a break but you also *deserve* one after all you've accomplished.

The honeymoon is the one part of the wedding that belongs to you and your now-husband and nobody else (unless, of course, you've eloped somewhere exotic, in which case the whole thing is just one big fat sexy romantic escape). It's a chance to catch up on much-needed post-nuptial sleep and, ahem, nookie. A brief escape after the wedding gives you and your fellow an opportunity to reflect together on all that's just happened and exchange stories from the event, and it affords a peaceful setting for the two of you to set a tone for your life together.

Lucky for you, of all the industries that cater to brides and grooms, travel is the one that has the most to offer to last-minute planners. Although popular places tend to book up during popular seasons, a ton of online and offline services will pair up spontaneous vacationers with tour companies, cruise lines, airlines, and hotels all anxious to fill every available slot. If you can be flexible about the nitty-gritty, not only will you get yourself a great honeymoon but you'll probably get it at a bargain.

Travel at the Speed of Web

Not only is going online a great way to find last-minute fares, but you can do your research and purchasing at night, freeing up days for meetings with caterers, florists, and other folks. A few things to keep in mind before you go online:

- Do your research! Knowing when and where you want to travel is key to saving time and money online. If you're not sure, you may want to talk it over with a travel agent who specializes in your destination.

- Visit airline Web sites first for last-minute fares. They often publish fares on their sites that aren't available elsewhere. From there, comparison shop on reputable travel sites. Start with your departure city, as most airfare discounts are listed according to departure locations.

- For packages and cruises, be sure to check out sites that specialize in getting great rates for last-minute vacationers. (See Resources at the end of this book.)

- Make sure your online travel site is reputable. Does it have a professional appearance? Has it been reviewed by the travel press? Do you know people who've used it? Few things are worse than discovering that you've handed over your hard-earned cash to a fraud.

- Planning your own trip from start to finish? Travel message boards are great resources for recommendations for the perfect B & B or warnings about must-avoid tourist traps from fellow travelers.

Consider the Minimoon

You may be starting graduate school, on the verge of giving birth or unable to break away from the office just now. If you're not going to be taking a couple of weeks off anytime soon, you may want to opt for the "minimoon." Lasting anywhere from one night to three, the minimoon is a brief getaway that enables you and your husband to catch your breath before returning to your active lifestyles. Easily planned, the minimoon usually takes place somewhere peaceful and secluded just a few hours from home.

Sticking Close to Home

Difficulty getting away isn't the only reason to stick close to home. There are also the stressful planning, expensive flights, and harried passport updates—and don't forget your visas—that go along with a faraway honeymoon. A prolonged stay at your favorite weekend getaway or secluded family cabin may be just what the doctor ordered. By going somewhere close by, you'll be spending more time relaxing together instead of standing in airport security lines and on street corners hailing cabs. And if you're looking for a honeymoon that's less about a vacation than simply quality time with your spouse, then keeping it local may be the way to go.

Vacation-Wedding Combo

Say you're planning a trip to Paris. Once there, you and your man will be dining by candlelight, drinking amazing wine, and, *ooh la la*, looking at the twinkling reflection of street lights on the Seine. He loves you. You love him. So what the hell? Get married while you're at it! While a destination wedding can be one that's planned to be just that, if you're planning a vacation, want to get married, and aren't interested in bothering with the whole huge wedding-planning thing, then use your vacation as an excuse to get married. And the honeymoon? Well, you'll be on it once you say, *"Oui oui."*

Nice Package

Travel packages and cruises may never qualify as the road less traveled, but they are certainly the easiest route. Plunking down one check in exchange for one easy itinerary means less planning and fewer details left to chance. With a package, you're entrusting the experts to handle the particulars so that you and your fellow can just show up and enjoy yourselves! Better yet, packages, cruises, and even tours are more likely to appear on Web sites that specialize in last-minute travel bargains.

Honeymoon Later

There is no hard-and-fast law that says you have to exit your wedding beneath a shower of birdseed and limo straightaway to the airport for some faraway destination. There's no reason you need to honeymoon right away at all. Sometimes just planning a wedding and getting married is enough for the time being. You may even decide to take a minimoon and save the bon voyage for a later date when you'll be far more able to appreciate it. If you're hoping to spend your honeymoon hiking the Himalayas, sailing around the world, or doing any other activity that might require a great deal of energy and planning, you may want to enjoy your wedding now and take your honeymoon after you've had some time to recover.

Two Weddings, One Couple

Things moved quickly from the beginning for Randy and Miza Reamer. In the summer of 1999, Randy, an American architect, had just ended a job in the Philippines and was about to move to San Francisco when he met Miza, a lawyer, at a bar during a visit to Malaysia. Sparks flew. They had a date, and then had another, and soon Randy was pushing back his trip to the States in order to spend more time with Miza. When he finally did leave, they agreed she'd join him in a couple of months and they would go for it. Two months later, they were living together in the City by the Bay, very much in love.

Randy says they felt immense pressure to get married from the beginning. "We both knew that things would be easier for us if we just got married, but we wanted it to be heartfelt. We didn't want to get engaged and married just because of the INS," he recalls. So they held off and just enjoyed themselves.

The following spring they vacationed in Mexico. Sometime during the trip, they decided to start planning a wedding when they got back home. But that day never arrived. Despite the fact that all of Miza's paperwork was in order, she was detained at the border, jailed, and deported to Malaysia. "Our attorneys advised me to move there. It was going to take years before she could come back into the States without getting married," Randy says. Within two weeks Randy had packed up their belongings and was on his way to join her in Malaysia. Less than a week after his arrival, he and Miza had a full-blown wedding.

One hundred and fifty of Miza's friends and relatives gathered at her aunt's house to celebrate and give traditional blessings, following a civil ceremony at a government office, according to Malaysian Muslim custom. Randy says putting together the big party in a hurry was easy. "In Malaysia, there are so many convention spaces and hotels, that there's not that need to book too far in advance. You can just call places up and say 'I need catering for two hundred people.' Miza's aunt got tents, tables, linens, caterers, and waiters with two phone calls," he explains. Planned and paid for by Miza's family, the wedding was the easy part. It took an entire year of legal wrangling and petitioning with congressional representatives before they were allowed to return to the States as a couple— and even that was amazingly fast for this type of process.

Once they'd settled back into life in the United States, it was time to plan another wedding, one of their own design, for their American friends and family. While still in Malaysia, they'd already found the location they wanted via the Internet, a house on a bluff overlooking the Pacific, and they knew they wanted to have the event

before daylight saving time began in late October. In July, they visited the spot. In late August they were able to get their finances together to book it for late October, leaving just two months to plan everything.

For wedding number two, Miza watched American movies featuring weddings in order to get a sense of how the "white wedding" worked. Miza's friend, a Malaysian fashion designer, made a traditional white gown for her, which she saw for the first time the day she would wear it. Randy bought a suit. They listened to music and burned CDs to play in lieu of hiring a DJ. One hundred invitations were rush ordered and hastily mailed, although the invitees had been informed of the date well in advance. Randy's sister, a florist, picked up flowers from the flower market and put together the arrangements. Email introductions and explanations of cultural expectations were sent to family members and guests, as the couple made extensive travel arrangements for Miza's relatives, most of whom had never been to the States.

"It was a seven-day-a-week thing. Every single night when we got home, it was either a discussion, an adventure, or an argument over these decisions that had to be made immediately," Randy recalls. "We were lucky because every decision was a financial one. It cut out a lot of superfluous stuff. We knew the minimum things we wanted and we did them the best we could."

They're still waiting to go on their honeymoon.

Last-Minute Details

PASSPORTS, VISAS, AND IMMIGRATION ISSUES If you plan
to travel out of the country, be sure that your passport is up-to-date.
Passport applications take an average of six weeks to process.
If you're in a hurry, you can apply in person and pay extra
fees to have your paperwork processed immediately,
though you will still need to wait a couple of weeks
for delivery. There are a number of private businesses that specialize in expediting passports in
24 hours. If you are not a citizen of the country
you're living in, be sure there's no extra paperwork
required of you for reentry.

KEEPING HEALTHY Getting sick is no fun, and
getting sick on your honeymoon really, truly sucks. Load up on vitamins
and water for travel of any distance. If you're heading somewhere
exotic, find out whether any immunizations or other precautions are
recommended. Keep in mind that some immunizations take several
weeks to kick in. Other treatments, such as that for malaria, continue
for several weeks after your trip and may have serious side effects.

CA-CHING! Business travelers and frequent adventurers may want
to take this opportunity to cash in their frequent-flier miles. Grabbing
a free flight frees up extra cash to spend on a boutique hotel or some
fancy dinners. Or, use your miles to upgrade to first class for this extra-
special vacation. Similarly, a frequent-flier friend or relative can
purchase your tickets using their miles as a great gift.

WEATHER REPORTS AND POLITICAL SITUATIONS It's no good
to arrive in the Bahamas during hurricane season or Central America in
the midst of a political uprising. Follow news and weather reports for
your chosen destination closely—preferably *before* booking flights and
lodging, but also afterward.

Marriage is the real adventure you're embarking on, and the honeymoon is just the icing on the cake. Whether you're jetting to some remote tropical island or backpacking in national parks or simply enjoying a quiet week at home with all phones and computers turned off, what matters is that you take a little time to reflect on all that's happened and unwind after all the craziness. Be together. That's what honeymooning is all about.

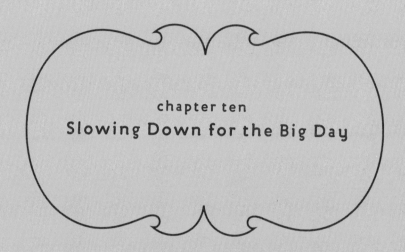

chapter ten
Slowing Down for the Big Day

Mantras! Write down all the happy reasons you're getting married.
Read them whenever you're feeling stressed.

❀ Slowing Down for the Big Day

One week to go...
Wrap things up at work.
Get plenty of exercise and rest.
One day to go...
Prepare yourself to have fun!

Putting together a wedding is always an exhausting, emotional, and transformative experience—whether the planning phase lasts a year or a week. There will always be something else to do. There *will* be nasty fights with friends, family, and, believe it or not, your sweetheart. Unexpected problems will arise and you'll have to deal with them on the spot. All this while juggling your career, social life, family, and pets. Pretty it ain't.

Being short on time shouldn't be one more reason for you to stress out. Rather, it's your excuse to take extra-special care of yourself and your relationship over the weeks or days leading up to the wedding. While there's no right or wrong way to unwind—everybody's different— there are some basic guidelines you can follow to ensure that you're healthy and happy and completely relaxed on your important day.

Easy Come, Easy Go

Planning a last-minute wedding means that you'll have to let go of some things you may have wanted. Compromises and sacrifices will be necessary. This is life. The less you fight and the quicker you let go and move on, the smoother your planning will be and the better you'll feel. When the day of your wedding arrives, you'll be amazed that so many things you worried over don't seem to matter at all.

Delegate

You'll receive many offers of help from friends and family. Even if you suspect they're just being nice, take them up on their contribution.

Assign everyone a task—from giving the caterer a check and making sure rentals are returned intact to bringing you pizza during your wedding-day beauty session. Make sure they understand what's expected of them, thank them sincerely, and then check the task off your list.

Skip the Diet

Skipping meals and counting calories will only make you tired, grumpy, and less able to deal with the wedding. In the worst-case scenario, a crash diet combined with the pressure of the impending wedding could get you sick and even hospitalized. The few inches you may manage to shed just aren't worth it. Trust your fiancé, who knows without doubt that you're the most beautiful creature on the planet, and save the diet for after you return from the honeymoon.

Don't Skip the Exercise

Exercise lowers stress, combats depression, makes you feel more energetic, reduces PMS, and burns unwanted fat. Any questions?
Oh, it can also be a nice way for you and your honey to spend some time
together. Plan to go running, hiking, or cycling together a couple times a week. Doing yoga or some kind of stretching once or twice a week will soothe your nerves and relax those poor tense muscles.

Different types of exercise produce different effects on your body and mental state. Get the most out of your workouts by matching your fitness routine to your mood.

Stressed out? Yoga relaxes the muscles as well as the mind. Make sure to find a class that begins with meditation and ends with a restorative pose.

Angry? Expend all that negative energy in a long run or spinning class.

Scattered? Regain focus with some tai chi, karate, or yoga instruction.

Depressed? Attending an ethnic dance class or spending a night at the clubs can chase those blues away.

Trapped? A hike or bike ride amid the splendor of nature will get you out of the house and remind you of how beautiful the world can be.

Low self-esteem? Do something sexy like taking a belly-dancing lesson or getting pampered with a massage and facial.

135

Work It Out

Let your employer and any clients or other affected parties know about your impending plans as soon as possible. If you can, hand over all-consuming projects to capable colleagues until after the wedding. Set aside lunch hours for making phone calls and meeting with caterers, florists, and other wedding pros. If you work for a progressive company, they'll probably let you take a few days off for planning, too.

Kill Two Birds

Have a romantic dinner with your fiancé at a place you're considering for the rehearsal dinner. Spend a fun Saturday wine tasting to choose the vintages for your reception. Invite friends to keep you company on shopping trips and other errands. Whenever possible, make your wedding activities fun and your fun activities wedding so you get ample time to do both.

But Don't Forget to Set Aside Nonwedding Time

The wedding can very easily take over your whole life and relationship, and that's not something you want. Set aside wedding-free periods (a day or an evening, depending on how much time you can spare) in which no plans may be made or even discussed.

Communicate Your Feelings

The talking cure can cure a lot, it turns out. If your mother-in-law is being a pain, don't bottle those feelings up until they explode. Tell her as nicely as you can to butt out (or, better yet, ask your betrothed to talk to her on your behalf). If your groom doesn't seem to be pulling his weight, don't suck it up; tell the man you need a little help here. Vent to girlfriends. Cry when you feel the need to cry, however irrational it may seem. A wedding is a very emotional thing. You'll have a lot to say and express during this time and the more you're able to let it out, the better you'll feel.

No, Your Fiancé Hasn't Been Replaced by an Alien

It never fails. You think you know someone inside and out, and then you plan a wedding and suddenly you find out what he or she *really* thinks about family, children, travel, and the institution of marriage. With the stakes so high, things can get nasty, fast. Many a case of cold feet begins after such an argument, but there's no need to freak out. Just remember that getting married is all part of this long, difficult, and rewarding growing process, and enjoy getting to know each other even better.

Live Happily Ever After

What more is there to say? If you've made it this far, you've got plenty to look forward to, and the sooner the better!

Resources

Dresses

Maternity Outfitters sells dressy gowns for pregnant wives-to-be.

www.maternityoutfitters.com

Even if you're not comfortable buying your wedding dress from a complete stranger online, eBay is a great source of bags, veils, shoes, jewelry, and other fun girly stuff.

www.ebay.com

Health and Body

Don't spend your wedding day worrying whether your tampon will hold up! Chart your cycle before you pick a date at sites like Cycles Page.

www.cyclespage.com

Immigration/Passports

The road to citizenship begins with the U.S. Immigration and Naturalization Service and U.S.A. Visas Immigration Services.

www.ins.gov

800-375-5283

www.usais.org

888-407-4747; from overseas, 1-317-472-2328

Need a passport? Start with the U.S. State Department Passport Services.

travel.state.gov/passport_services.html

900-225-5674

888-362-8668

Invitations

Companies like Wedding Invitations 411 can ship within a week.

www.weddinginvitations411.com

877-645-2793

Legal

Nolo Press's books and Web site are chock-a-block with expert advice on everything from the legal effects of marriage to managing changes in tax status.

www.nolo.com

800-728-3555

Locations

Avoid "wedding mills" by turning to your local chamber of commerce instead. Go to chamber-of-commerce.com, or check local listings.

GayWeddings.com is your one-stop shop for Vermont wedding licenses, same-sex cake toppers, gay wedding planners, and open-minded honeymoon hotels.

www.gayweddings.com

Vicki's Vegas wedding packages can be found at www.lvweddingsbyvicki.com. For more options and information on Nevada legal marriage requirements, visit www.ci.las-vegas.nv.us.

Marriage Licenses/Officiants

For instant ordination, you'll want to contact the Universal Life Church or the Church of Spiritual Humanism.

www.ulc.org

2159 South Sky Tanner Drive

Tucson, AZ 85748

520-721-2882

www.spiritualhumanism.org

P.O. Box 180

Jenkintown, PA 19046

206-457-1966

The Knot has extensive information on obtaining marriage licenses, complete with state-by-state guides.

www.theknot.com

Music

You don't need a CD burner to create custom CDs. Companies like Total Media, Inc., let you select from a list of songs and choose from a menu of designs.

www.totalmediainc.com/custom_cds.htm

888-456-DISK

Photographers

Trade associations like The Wedding Bureau are a good place to begin a search for a wedding photographer.

www.weddingbureau.com

Planning

The Knot and The Wedding Channel are two leading wedding Web sites, with plenty of helpful information, tools, and business listings to get you on your way.

www.theknot.com

www.weddingchannel.com

If traditional wedding magazines and Web sites make you want to hurl yourself in front of the nearest commuter bus, IndieBride.com may provide just the kind of moral support you're looking for.

www.indiebride.com

EZ Wedding Planner's free software lets you keep track of your budget, while keeping all your addresses, seating information, and other files in one place.

www.ezweddingplanner.com

Tech Support

The Knot and WeddingChannel.com have easy-to-use Web-page builders. Just plug in the information, press send, and you've got a wedding Web site.

www.theknot.com

www.weddingchannel.com

Dreamweaver and Microsoft Front Page are two software programs that help experienced computer users create a Web page from scratch.
www.microsoft.com
www.dreamweaver.com

Traveling

Avoid sickness abroad by consulting with the National Center for Infectious Diseases Travelers' Health on your destination.
www.cdc.gov/travel

11th Hour Vacations specializes in last-minute bargains for travelers.
www.11thhourvacations.com

Site 59's expertise is in booking last-minute weekend trips.
www.site59.com

Lowestravel offers last-minute discounts on international flights.
www.lowestravel.com

Last Minute Travel displays last-minute discounts from several other online travel sites.
www.lastminutetravel.com

Not sure where to go? Lonely Planet's Thorn Tree is a top-notch travel bulletin board with recommendations and warnings from fellow globe-trotters.
www.thorntree.lonelyplanet.com

Weather

Stormfax Weather Almanac lets you see what the weather's been like on your wedding date in the past, while weather.com provides storm warnings and other helpful current information.
www.stormfax.com/almanac.htm
www.weather.com

Wedding Planners

Trade organizations like the Association of Bridal Consultants and June Wedding screen members to make sure they're top-notch. These organizations should be your first stop if you're thinking of hiring a planner.

www.bridalassn.com

860-355-0464

www.junewedding.com

702-474-9558

Index